STRING ART:
STEP-BY-STEP

STRING ART: STEP-BY-STEP

ROBERT E. SHARPTON

Chilton Book Company   Radnor, Pennsylvania

Library of Congress Cataloging in Publication Data

Sharpton, Robert E
    String Art: step-by-step

    (Chilton's creative crafts series)
    1. String craft. I. Title.
TT880.S53   746'.04'71   75-4191
ISBN 0-8019-6131-9
ISBN 0-8019-6132-7 pbk.

TO MY PARENTS

Beauty is Nature's brag, and must be shown
In courts, at feasts, and high solemnities,
Where most may wonder at the workmanship;
It is for homely features to keep home,
They had their name thence; coarse complexions
And cheeks of sorry grain will serve to ply
The sampler, and to tease the huswife's wool.
What need a vermeil-tinctur'd lip for that,
Love-darting eyes, or tresses like the morn?
COMUS, *John Milton*

Acknowledgments

I am grateful to my many patrons who showed great concern and admiration for my string design pieces over the years within the United States and abroad. I am especially thankful for the press coverage by journalists in the Miami area for introducing my work to educators and the community.

Individually, my deepest appreciation is extended to Ms. Margaria Fichtner of the Miami Herald Newspaper, Mr. Chris Warren Christman of the Dade County Parks and Recreation Department and Ms. Sally Jessy, of Channel 10 television station, Miami.

Special thanks to Mr. and Mrs. Bruce Miller, Miami, for sharing their home for some interior settings and Mr. Charles L. McIntyre for his photographic assistance.

I would also like to thank my colleagues, friends, and my students who over the years have helped me to make this project a reality for all ages. Sincere thanks to those who have viewed and shared criticism regarding my designs, for without their advice this publication could not have been a book designed for everyone.

Finally, I wish to thank my editor Crissie Lossing for giving me the opportunity to share this experience with everyone. Her evaluation of my previous works and publications served as a basis for the organization of this book.

Contents

List of Illustrations

List of Color Illustrations

Introduction

Today, more than ever before, people are seeking ways to relax and to express their creativity. String art (or string sculpture, as it is sometimes called) is one of the fastest growing hobbies in the world. However, it is not a totally new form of expression. Ever since man learned to spin fibers into thread and weave thread to make fabric, an infinite number of useful and decorative items have been created.

Historically, thread, yarn, and rope have played a significant role. During the primitive era they were used in hunting, fishing, and making clothing and as supports in the construction of shelter. In the mid 1700s, string was employed artistically in "curve stitching." A design was outlined on a piece of heavy paper similar to cardboard and then holes were punched in the paper and numbered. Using a needle and thread, the individual created a string design by following the numbered holes. Curve stitching is still present today in children's sewing cards.

In more recent times, curve stitching has been used to motivate learning in the field of mathematics by helping students to visualize mathematic and geometric concepts. Early European teachers, constantly looking for ways to motivate and assist children in the difficult area of abstract concepts, successfully used curve stitching to fight fatigue in the classroom.

Beginning in the early 1900s, educators sought ways to improve teaching methods in the more structured disciplines such as mathematics. Soon after, several publications on geometric designs and patterns appeared in the Soviet Union and "A Rhythmic Approach to Mathematics" was published in Central Europe in 1906.

And yet, through the years, few teachers of mathematics or art have pursued the usage of string as a medium to bridge the gap between the arts and mathematics.

In the United States, the art of stringing pictures came to the fore in the late 1960s and 1970s. The acceptance of string design as an art form has been slow—even though there were several outstanding string compositions in well-known museums throughout the world.

Since the early 1960s, I have used string pictures as a learning tool in my mathematics classes. I have noticed a positive and significant change in the students' attitude toward mathematics, and a considerable amount of interest has been shown by all those actively involved in the experience. I have taught string art to children and adults of all ages and educational levels both in the United States and abroad. Their response has given me a spark of hope.

My mathematics students here at Miami-Dade Community College have developed and created elementary string pictures within a short period of time without becoming totally involved in the mathematics of their designs. More intricate stringing patterns are developed as they learn the more difficult geometric concepts.

The projects herein do not require a mathematic approach. Simply enjoy the shapes, colors, and textures and then use these examples as a basis for your own creative designs.

STRING ART:
STEP-BY-STEP

Tools
and
Materials

As a beginner in the craft of stringing pictures, you will probably prefer to make your first effort on a simple design such as any basic shape found around the home or in the environment. Such designs are readily available and can easily be made into string pictures with a little knowledge of shapes and thread patterns.

Most string pictures for the beginner are worked with one shape and one or two colors of threads. There is no reason why your first finished piece can't be attractive, and it is sure to give you a sense of personal satisfaction!

The tools and materials required for making string pictures are available in local department stores, craft and hobby shops, hardware stores, lumberyards, and variety stores. Figures 1, 2, 3, and 4 show many of the supplies required.

The cost of your tools will vary according to brand names and according to the material of which the tool is made (metal, wood, or

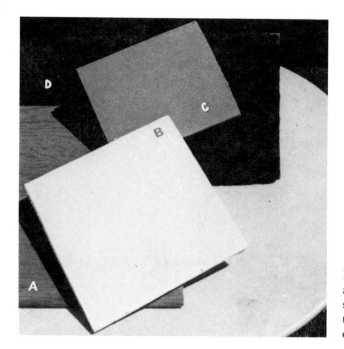

Figure 1 Types of woods and surface boards for designs. A, plywood; B, ceiling tile; C, lightweight lumber; D, corkboard.

Figure 2 Your background board can be covered with fabric as indicated on board 1 or can be painted as shown on board 2.

Figure 3   Background fabrics (cotton, velvet, burlap, or silk), thread, yarn, sewing thread, nylon filament, wire, and knitting yarns used in string art.

Figure 4 Hammer, saw, protractor, triangle, and T-square are some of the tools you may use.

3

plastic). In any case, the same high quality of work can be achieved regardless of the cost of the materials.

Choosing Your Board

Your background board should be ¼" to 1" thick. Some of the boards which can be used include *plywood, flakeboard* (chipboard), *corkboard, lightweight lumber, homosote®,* or *ceiling tile.*

Plywood is material made of layers of wood glued tightly together; the grains are usually joined at right angles to each other. Flakeboard is material made of wood chips and sawdust pressed tightly together. It is a little heavy for portable wall designs. Corkboard is material made of compressed and baked granules of cork. Homosote board is material made of pressed paper and is excellent for string designs.

Selecting Background Fabric and Thread

Background fabric is one of the most important items in string art. The fabric you choose will enhance or destroy your design. The art of stringing pictures is a total look at the design, background fabric, thread, and threading pattern. Texture is also very important. Once you have decided on a particular design or pattern, it's important to keep the room decor and the pattern itself in mind.

Most often felt is the best background fabric for string pictures. Certainly it is the best fabric for beginners. Generally speaking, any background fabric will work if it is firmly attached to the board and if the thread or threads used to create the design are suited to the texture of the fabric.

If you should select a cotton background fabric, then cotton thread would be the best choice. If you are working with velvet or velour fabric, then silks and polyesters would be best.

You will be able to use cotton threads of varying thicknesses on fabrics such as burlap, denim, sailcloth, and the woven weaves. For example, if the design is placed on burlap, cotton or knitting thread is preferable. The completed string design will have a textured look that will complement the background. If a silk or polyester thread is used on burlap, the threading pattern will have to be repeated several times in order for the string design to stand out from the coarse burlap.

Remember, if you are using a heavy or bulky fabric, you need to use a heavy-looking thread. If you are using a softer and more delicate background fabric, then you will want a delicate thread.

Fabrics	*Suggested Threads*
Cotton twill, dobby, burlap, union cloth, velvet, denim, sailcloth	Mercerized sewing threads, cottons Heavy duty mercerized sewing threads Heavy duty sewing threads with polyester Super sheen cotton threads Acrylic yarns Darning cottons Cable cord Heavy duty nylon cord (rope) Embroidery threads Macrame yarns and cords Nylon monofilament (fishing line) Knitting yarns
Velvet, felt (60% rayon, 40% wool; 50% wool, 50% rayon)	Polyester sewing threads Cotton threads Silk threads (single or twist) Acrylic yarns Copper wire Nylon sewing threads Embroidery threads Metallic threads (lame)

Suitable velvets include velours and velveteens; don't use crushed velvet or corduroy velvet. If you choose to work with copper wire, use a gauge that is suitable for your design and flexible for stringing it tight; it is also recommended that you wear gloves to avoid burns and cuts while working with wire.

Buying Brads

Brads are tapered nails with small heads or a slight side projection instead of a head. The length of the brads you use will depend on the thickness of your board.

For most designs, you will want to use brads ½″ or ⅝″ in length. However, if your board is 1″ or thicker, you may then use a 1½″ brad. Or, if the design you are working calls for several threading layers, then you will probably want to use a 1″ brad.

All of the projects in this book can be worked with galvanized brads. These brads are greyish in color and blend easily with all threads and backgrounds. They are sold in boxes by weight and are relatively low in cost.

Brass brads known as "escutcheon pins" are usually used on the better quality fabrics such as velour, velvet, and the weaves. Otherwise the overall effect is not achieved.

Gathering Supplies

Many of the supplies you need for making string art pictures are common household items:

fabric glue—Sobo® or Elmer's®, for attaching fabric to board; used in place of staples; not suggested for use on velvet or velour
hammer—for pounding brads into board to form your design
masking tape—for holding pattern onto board
pens and pencils—for making your pattern
ruler—for measuring distances and marking brad placement
sandpaper—for smoothing edges of your board
scissors—for cutting fabric
tweezers—for pulling the string through the brads

Many supplies can be purchased at your local hardware store:

staple gun and staples—for attaching fabric to board; used in place of fabric glue; strongly suggested for use on velvet or velour
paints, stains, and brushes—for finishing board; used in place of background fabric.

The rest of the supplies can be purchased in a craft or hobby or art supply store:

compass—for drawing circles
graph paper—for enlarging or reducing patterns
protractor—if you wish to work the circular designs in degrees rather than inches
tracing paper—for making your design pattern

Techniques and Procedures

Beginning and Ending a Project

Figure 5 Select your board, background fabric, and brads. To cover the board, you will need scissors, fabric glue or staples, and masking tape. You will need a ruler or yardstick to position the pattern on the board and measure the brad depth. The edges of the board should be sanded smooth and the corners must be clean. Cut your fabric about 1½″ to 2″ wider and longer than the board size. For example, if the board measures 16″ × 24″, cut the fabric 18″ × 26″. This will allow sufficient fabric for folding it over the board.

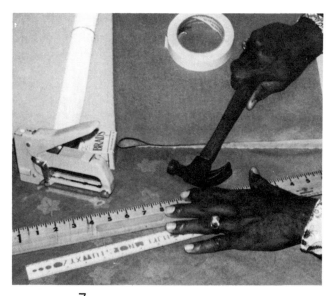

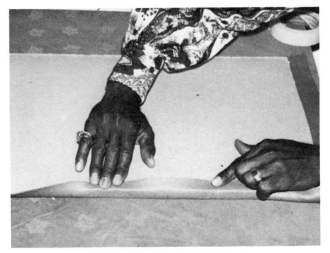

Figure 6 Place the wrinkle-free fabric face down on a hard, flat surface such as a table or the floor. Now place your board in the center of the fabric. Fold the fabric edge over the board and place a piece of masking tape at each corner and in the center of each side to temporarily hold the fabric in position. As you work, pull the fabric tight from one side to the other to prevent air spaces under the fabric.

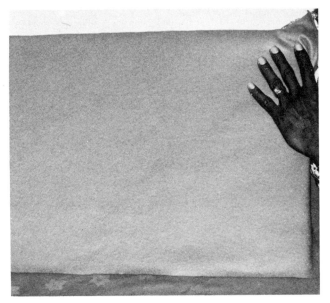

Figure 7 After checking the front for wrinkles and making sure the corner folds haven't caused puckers, glue or staple the fabric to the back of the board. Attach one side and then check to make sure that the fabric is smooth and taut before attaching the other sides. (If you are using a velvet or velour background fabric, use gloves to avoid leaving heavy fingerprints on the surface. Extra care must be taken when placing brads in velvet and velour. This sort of background fabric is expensive and is not recommended for beginners.)

Figure 8 Place your pattern on the covered board and put masking tape on each corner to hold it in position. Using a hammer, place the brads in the marked positions. The brads will usually be ¼″ apart. At least one-quarter or one-half of the brad should remain above the surface of the board. Measure the brads as you hammer them into the board so that they will all be the same height.

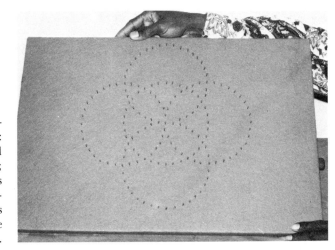

Figure 9 Remove the pattern from the covered board: gently lift the paper upward so as not to tear the pattern; pattern will have brad holes but can be used again if carefully removed. Inspect brads to make sure they are secure and in their proper positions.

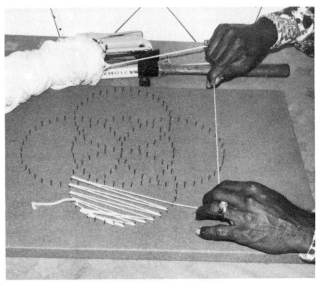

Figure 10 To thread the pattern, find the starting position, knot the thread around the brad, and follow the step-by-step directions for your project. Make sure to keep the thread taut as you work. Tie off by knotting the thread around the last brad. Cut off the excess, leaving about ½″ loose; coat the end with clear nail polish or fabric glue and wrap it around the brad.

Figure 11 Select a frame that will not detract from the string design.

Figure 12 The completed project shown here has been suitably framed and is ready for hanging.

Adapting Designs for Stringing

There are two fundamental methods of adapting designs. The first is for designs which are the exact size you wish to use for your pattern. The second method is for enlargement or reduction of a given design.

The first method requires little skill: simply cut a piece of pattern paper the same size as the board surface; arrange the design on the pattern, according to the basic principles of design such as balance and proportion; sketch or copy the design, using tracing paper, onto the pattern paper.

The second method, enlarging or reducing a design, can be achieved by the grid system and is worked on graph paper. To *reduce a design,* divide the original into 2″ squares with a ruler and pencil. You now have a grid effect over the design. Using ½″ or 1″ graph paper (depending on how much you want to reduce the design), transfer the design line by line and square by square. If you transfer the design to 1″ graph paper, your design will be one-half the size of the original. If you transfer the design to ½″ graph paper, it will be one-fourth the size of the original.

To enlarge a pattern, use this same grid technique in reverse. For example, draw a ½″ grid on the original and transfer the design to graph paper with 1″ or 2″ grids. Your pattern will now be two or four times larger than the original, depending on which size graph paper you used.

Remember, if the completed design is to be two, three, or four times larger than the original, each square on your final pattern must be two, three, or four times larger than the grid on the original.

If you plan to use your design pattern several times, it might be helpful to make your final pattern on a piece of cardboard or posterboard.

10

Basic Threading Patterns

Figure 13a *Horizontal threading* patterns are worked as follows: Tie your thread at brad 1 and pull directly across to the number 1 on opposite side; loop around and drop down to brad 2 on the same side; loop around and pull across to brad 2 on the opposite side. (All brads on the same side of the board will have a link between them.)

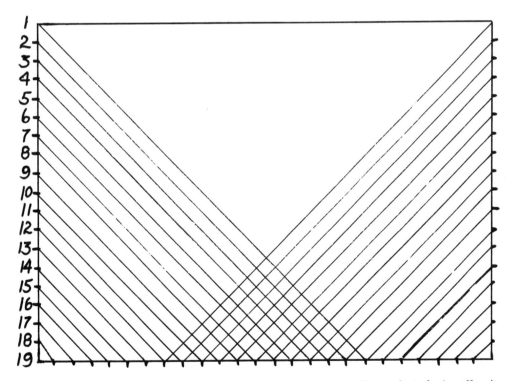

Figure 13b Here the horizontal threading is worked on a diagonal. A *lattice effect* is achieved where diagonal lines are overlapped.

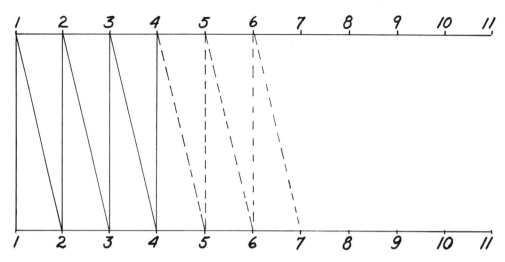

Figure 14   The *diagonal threading* pattern is the basic *one-to-one correspondence method.*

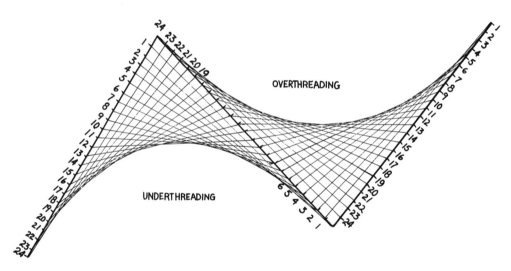

Figure 15   *Underthreading and overthreading* patterns can be used with both straight line designs and curved line designs. They are also one-to-one correspondence methods

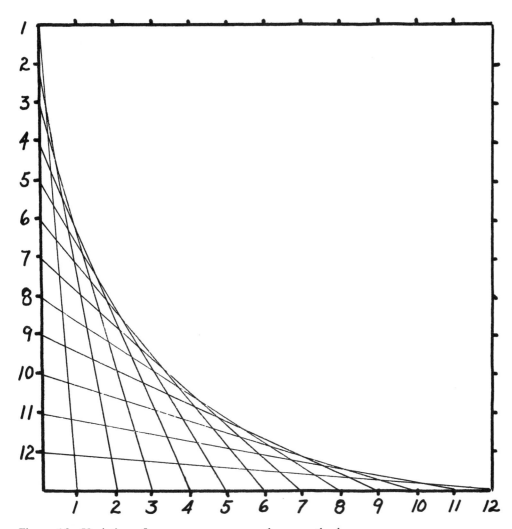

Figure 16   Variation of one-to-one correspondence method

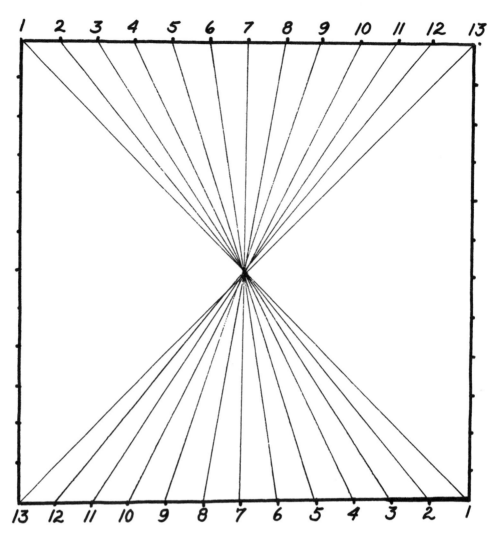

Figure 17   Variation of one-to-one correspondence method known as the *twisting thread pattern*

Choosing and Finishing Frames

The selection of a suitable frame for your string picture is of tremendous importance. The same care should be taken in selecting a frame for your string piece as when selecting your background fabric and thread. The type of frame selected will certainly make a difference in the appearance of the finished wall hanging. Frames made of the same kind of material and shape but finished in different ways can change the total appearance of the string picture.

Some string pictures are more functional without a frame while others are more appealing with a frame. The type of background fabric often dictates whether or not a frame is necessary. If a soft delicate fabric such as velvet or silk is used, than a frame would serve

14

as a protector as well as a complement to the piece. On the other hand, if a heavy or bulky textured fabric such as burlap is used or if a cotton background of a dark color is used, then the string piece could be left without a frame. In some cases, if the design is extremely delicate, the picture may be framed and then placed under glass.

A few general definitions of wood finish will help you select frames for your string pictures:

Wood finish—light, medium, or dark oils used mainly on canewood, maplewood, walnut, and other hardwoods whose grain is highly enhanced by using it.

Lacquer finish—used to give a high gloss to the surface, wood or metal.

Teak finish—used when black is required, but where a lacquer coat would be too hard. Black alcohol stain is used with cotton and a coat of clear lacquer is sprayed. Then a quick drying black varnish, known as Black Japan, is wiped on with a cotton cloth and the excess removed. When setting has taken place, add another coat of lacquer. Black Japan is available at large craft stores and art supply stores.

Wood stains—available at paint shops and large department stores. These are stains that will darken as more is applied. The degree of color depends on the number of coats used, and the degree to which the wood soaks up the stain.

Leafing—is a specialized technique. This type of finishing is expensive and unless your design is of excellent quality in design and fabric, I would not recommend leafing.

Antiquing—instruction is easily obtained and can be achieved reasonably well at minimum cost by a beginner.

Spatter—an excellent finish, using an assortment of inks. Secure a brush with stiff bristles and dip into the ink. Hold the brush at an angle and about 5 to 8 inches from the frame. Hit the brush against a hard handle to permit ink spots to fall on the surface. This process should be done quickly and evenly to avoid running drops.

The following is a list of some of the standard frame sizes:

8 × 10 inches	12 × 16 inches	20 × 24 inches
9 × 12 inches	14 × 18 inches	22 × 28 inches
10 × 12 inches	16 × 20 inches	24 × 30 inches
11 × 14 inches	18 × 24 inches	

Be sure to secure proper hooks on the frame for hanging according to the size and weight of your picture.

Working with Colors

From the beginning of civilization, people have been attracted by colors and have used color to reflect their personalities, wearing apparels, and homes.

A general understanding of the characteristics of color is important in developing your ability to appreciate colors and use them successfully in your designs. Observe the color spectrum as represented in Figure 18.

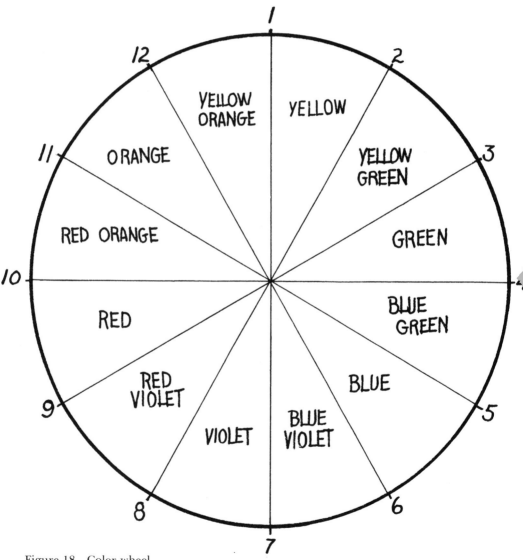

Figure 18   Color wheel.

Colors are classified under two major headings: *primary colors* are those which cannot be produced or developed by the blending of other colors; *secondary colors* are those on the color wheel which are equally spaced between two primary colors and are produced by the blending of primary colors. The primary colors are red, yellow, and blue. The secondary colors include orange, made of red and yellow; green, made of yellow and blue; purple, made of blue and red.

Those colors directly opposite each other on the color wheel are called *complimentary colors*. Complimentary colors provide beautiful and harmonious contrasts: red with green, yellow with purple, blue with orange.

When designing your string pieces, it is important to consider your thread color or colors along with your background fabric color as well as the room color. You can better visualize the overall appearance of your design by trying a mixture of threads on the background fabric. Threads such as the variegated ones and the various yarns used in knitting are helpful in providing lighter and darker tones to a design.

Color experimentation will provide great personal satisfaction to the finished piece, even if some of the general color guidelines are broken. If you are doubtful about a color scheme, use a monochromatic one. A *monochromatic color scheme* is made of tones of any one color. This is generally a tasteful way to enhance a room without the addition of too many colors.

Straight Line Flower

The beginner can become familiar with the one-to-one correspondence threading pattern and the use of the straight line by working this practice design. The lines of the flower can be of any length; each of the six lines which form the flower itself must be the same length. All brads should be spaced at least ¼″ apart; the center brad is left unthreaded.

The thread pattern used here is identical to the one-to-one threading pattern illustrated in Figure 14. Each line segment illustrated here has 14 points. (Fig. 19).

Making Your Design a Pattern

Using the pattern in Figure 19, draw or trace the outline for this design. Label each line segment of the flower 1 to 6 as shown; label each brad 1 to 14. Now label the brad points on the stem A to X. The brads on the leaves are labeled 1 to 18 and 1 to 19 (see Fig. 19).

Working the Threading Pattern

For the flower, tie thread at brad 1 on line 1, pull tight to brad 1 on line 2; loop around and return to brad 2 on line 1; loop around and return to brad 2 on line 2; and follow this sequence: 2-3; 3-3; 3-4; 4-4; 4-5; 5-5; 5-6; 6-6; 6-7; 7-7; 7-8; 8-8; 8-9; 9-10; 10-10; 11-11; 11-12; 12-12; 12-13; 13-13; 13-14; 14-14. Tie off.

Following the threading pattern above, thread line 2 with line 3, line 3 with line 4, line 4 with line 5, line 5 with line 6, line 6 with line 1 (see Fig. 20).

Note: when threading line 2 with line 3, brad 14 on line 2 becomes brad 1; brad 13 on line 2 becomes brad 2, and so on.

To thread the leaves and stems, work the stem on the right side A to 18; 18-B; B-17; 17-C; C-16; 16-D; D-15; 15-E; E-14; 14-F; F-13;

18

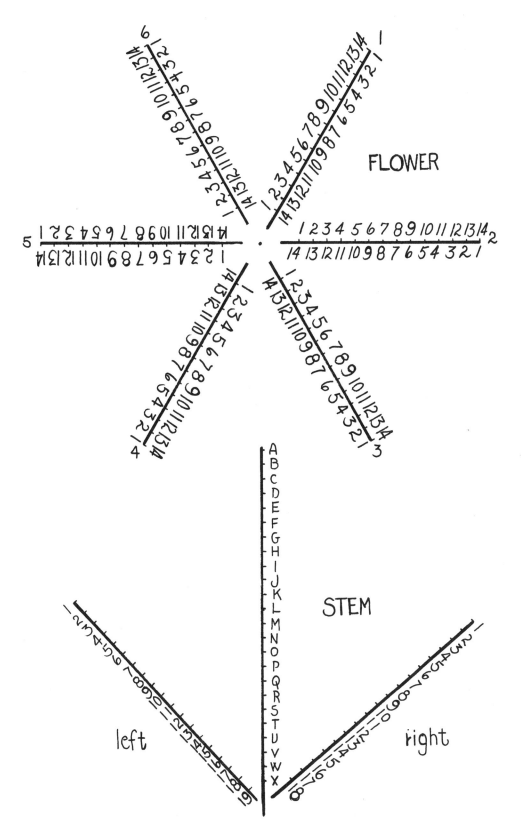

Figure 19 Straight Line Flower design pattern.

19

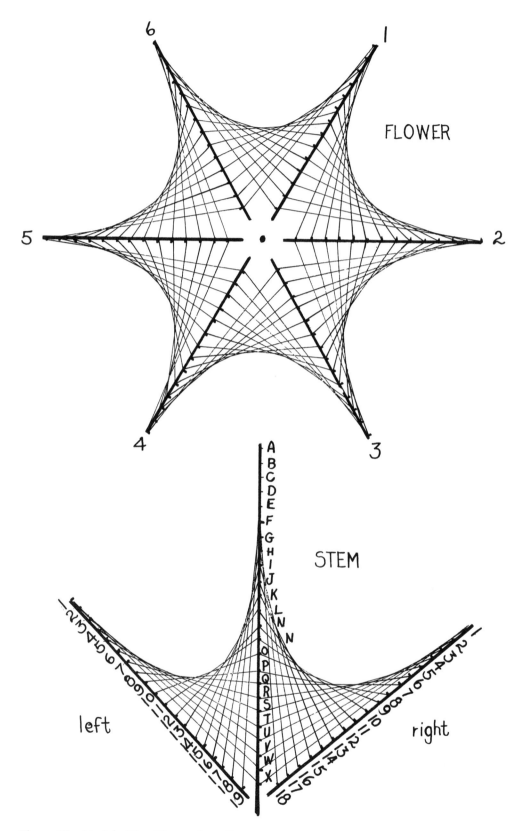

Figure 20   Straight Line Flower threading pattern.

13-G; G-12; 12-H; H-11; 11-I; I-10; 10-J; J-9; 9-K; K-8; 8-L; L-7; 7-M; M-6; 6-N; N-5; 5-O; O-4; 4-P; P-3; 3-Q; Q-2; 2-R; R-1. Tie off. On the left side, match A with 19; 19-B; B-18; 18-C; C-17; 17-D; D-16; 16-E; E-15; 15-F; F-14; 14-G; G-13; 13-H; H-12; 12-I; I-11; 11-J; J-10; 10-K; K-9; 9-L; L-8; 8-M; M-7; 7-N; N-6; 6-O; O-5; 5-P; P-4; 4-Q; Q-3; 3-R; R-2; 2-S; S-1. Tie off.

Web

This is a string composition of straight lines (Fig. 21). All lines are of the same length, meet at the center point, and have the same number of brads.

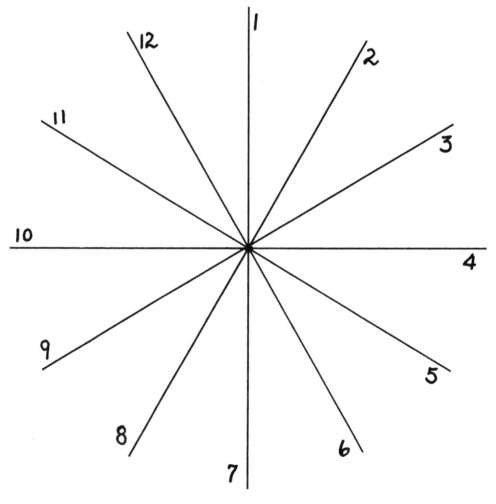

Figure 21   Web design pattern.

This design is excellent for either a square or rectangular shaped board. The lines may be of any length with brads at least ¼ inch apart. The threading pattern is interesting and pleasing to the eye.

Approximately 225 to 250 yards of sewing thread are required for the project shown here. The overall dimensions of the board used here are 16″ × 24″; the design itself is 16″ × 16″. The brads are placed about ¼″ apart.

Figure 21 shows the inner section of the full-size Web pattern. Note the numbering of brads 1 to 19 in Figure 3-4; number your brads consecutively, using this illustration as a guide.

The design is modern and can be strung with two different colors of thread or with one color. If you wish to work with two colors, lines

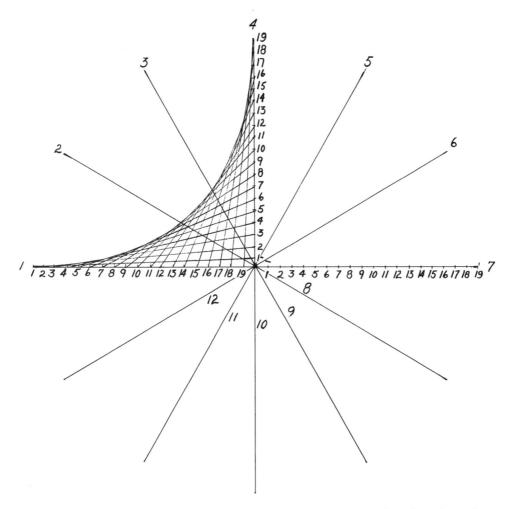

Figure 22   Web line 1 with line 4 threading pattern. Lines 8 through 12 have been shortened for purposes of illustration.

1-4, 4-7, 7-10, and 10-1 would be strung with one color; all the others would be strung with the second color. If you're working with one color, the background fabric should be a good contrast with your string.

To make the project shown here in the color section, you will need medium blue felt for the background; dark blue polyester thread for stringing lines 1-4, 4-7, 7-10, and 10-1; and light blue polyester thread for stringing the remaining sections.

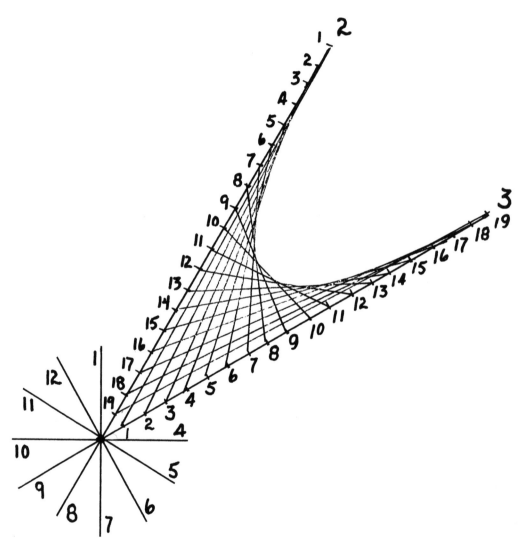

Figure 23   Web line 2 with line 3 threading pattern. All other lines have been shortened for purposes of illustration.

Making Your Design Pattern

To enlarge the pattern for this design, trace Figure 21 and extend lines 1 to 12 to 10″ (as in the project shown here) or to whatever length you wish to work. Now number the lines 1 to 12, following the pattern in Figure 22.

Working the Threading Pattern

The threading pattern for this project is the one-to-one correspondence method: string from brad 1 to brad 1; 1-2; 2-2; 2-3; 3-3; 3-4; 4-4; 4-5; 5-5; 5-6; 6-6; 6-7; 7-7; 7-8; 8-8; 8-9; 9-9; 9-10; 10-10; 10-11;

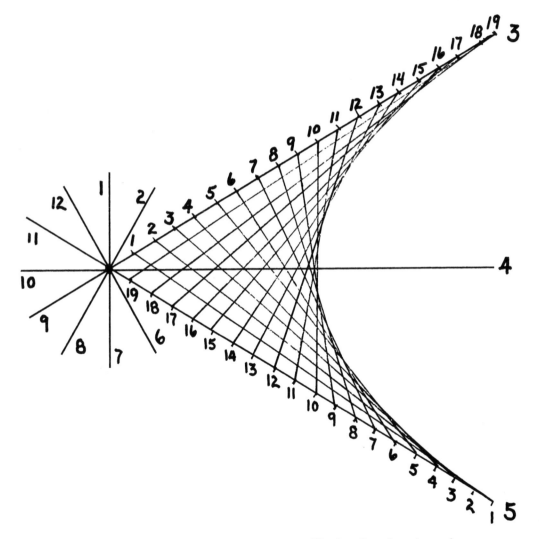

Figure 24 Web line 3 with line 5 threading pattern. All other lines have been shortened for purposes of illustration.

11-12; 12-12; 12-13; 13-13; 13-14; 14-14; 14-15; 15-15; 15-16; 16-16; 16-17; 17-17; 17-18; 18-18; 18-19; 19-19; and so on. Tie off.

Note: The center brad is not involved in the threading pattern; it is left free of thread.

1.   Begin by working this threading pattern as follows: line 1 with line 4 (Fig. 22); line 4 with line 7; line 7 with line 10; line 10 with line 1. Tie off.

2.   Now thread line 2 with line 3 (Fig. 23); line 3 with line 5 (Fig. 24); line 5 with line 6; line 6 with line 8; line 8 with line 9; line 9 with line 11; line 11 with line 12; line 12 with line 2. Tie off.

As you move from section to section, the numbering of the brads changes. For example, after you thread line 1 with line 4 and are ready to thread the next section, brad 19 (or your last brad) on line 4 becomes brad 1 for threading line 4 with line 7.

Follow the one-to-one correspondence method (1-1; 1-2; 2-2; 2-3 . . . 18-19; 19-19) until all lines are strung.

Soaring Seagulls

This is a string composition of straight lines, using the design elements of balance and proportion (Fig. 25). The design shown here

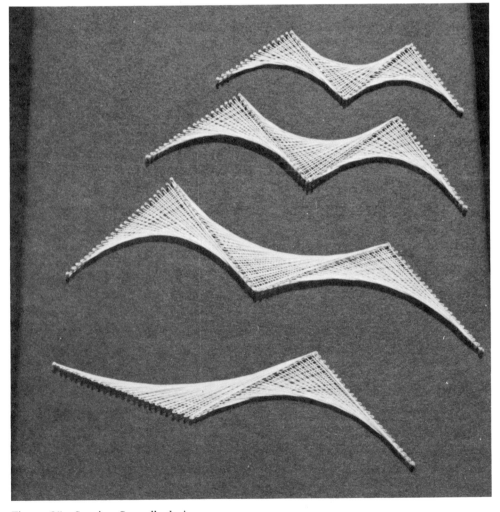

Figure 25   Soaring Seagulls design.

(with overall dimensions of 15″ × 15″) was worked on a vertical board (16″ × 24″) with a light shade of blue felt and the seagulls were strung with white cotton crochet thread.

Making Your Design Pattern

Using Figure 26 as a guide, draw the outlines for seagulls A, B, C, and D. Follow the approximate measurements and all brad numbering on Figure 26. All brads should be placed about ¼″ apart.

Working the Threading Pattern

The pattern used here is a one-to-one correspondence threading pattern. The same threading method is used for each seagull; the

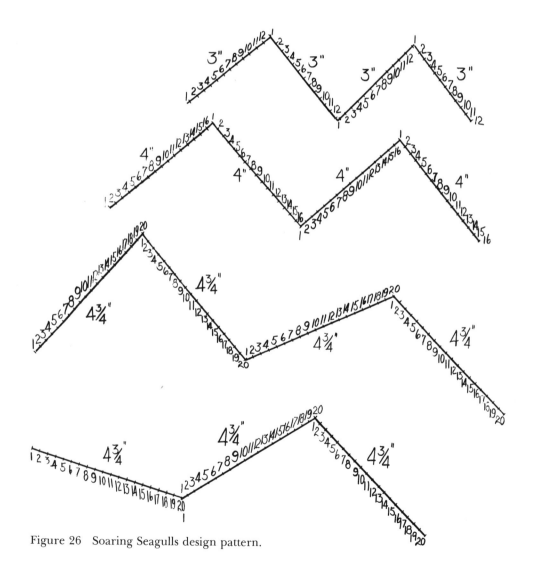

Figure 26   Soaring Seagulls design pattern.

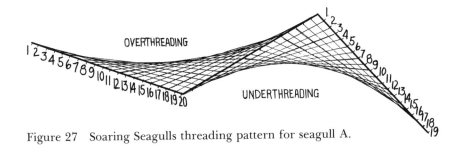

Figure 27   Soaring Seagulls threading pattern for seagull A.

only difference is in the number of brads in each line (see Fig. 26).

Refer to Figures 15 and 26 for the one-to-one correspondence, overthreading and underthreading patterns.

Seagulls A and B are threaded with 20 brads on each line (see Figs. 27 and 28); seagull C is threaded with 16 brads on each line; seagull D is threaded with 12 brads on each line (see Fig. 28).

Note: These seagulls may also be worked on a horizontal board and spaced in any form to satisfy your personal tastes.

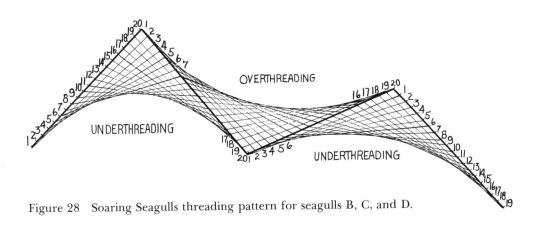

Figure 28   Soaring Seagulls threading pattern for seagulls B, C, and D.

Rectangular Spy

This is a unique and unusual string composition of four rectangles worked within a larger rectangle (Fig. 29). The threading is all worked with the one-to-one correspondence method. Rectangles A, B, and C are threaded alike; rectangle D is worked on opposite lines.

Starting at different points and threading various sides of the rectangle, you can achieve many different patterns (Figs. 30, 31 and 32). Your selection of colors can give this design an unusual appearance and can create a mysterious effect.

The overall dimension of this design as shown in the color section is 20" × 14"; the overall dimension of the board it was worked on is 22" × 30".

I worked this design on a green velvet background and strung it with shades of yellow, orange, purple, blue, and red threads. The frame has been painted with yellow enamel. The design can be hung horizontally or vertically for two totally different effects.

Making Your Design Pattern

Using Figure 29 as a guide, draw the overall rectangle 20" × 14". Now divide the rectangle into four smaller rectangles, each 10" × 7". Label these rectangles A, B, C, and D.

All brads should be placed about ¼" apart and should be labeled as shown in Figure 29.

Working the Threading Pattern

1. Using Figure 30 as a guide, thread the left and bottom lines of rectangle A with the one-to-one correspondence method. Tie your thread at brad 1 on the bottom line and pull to brad 28 on the left line and work as follows: 28-2; 2-27; 27-3; 3-26; 26-4; 4-25; 25-5; 5-24 . . . and so on.

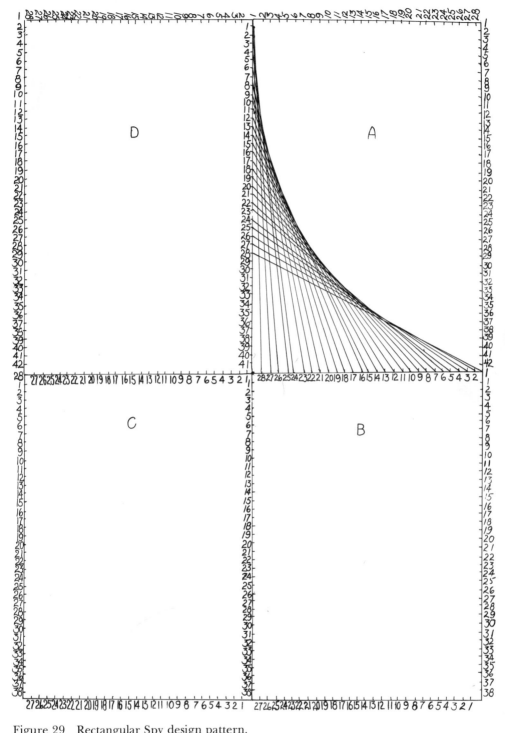

Figure 29 Rectangular Spy design pattern.

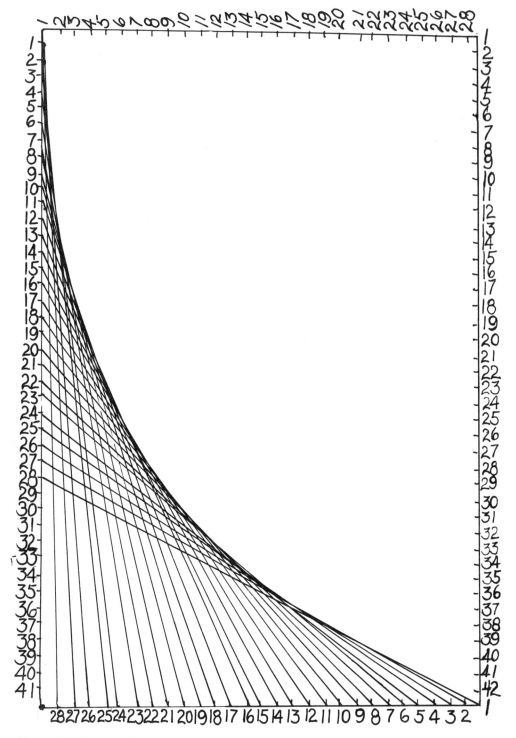

Figure 30   Rectangular Spy threading, step 1.

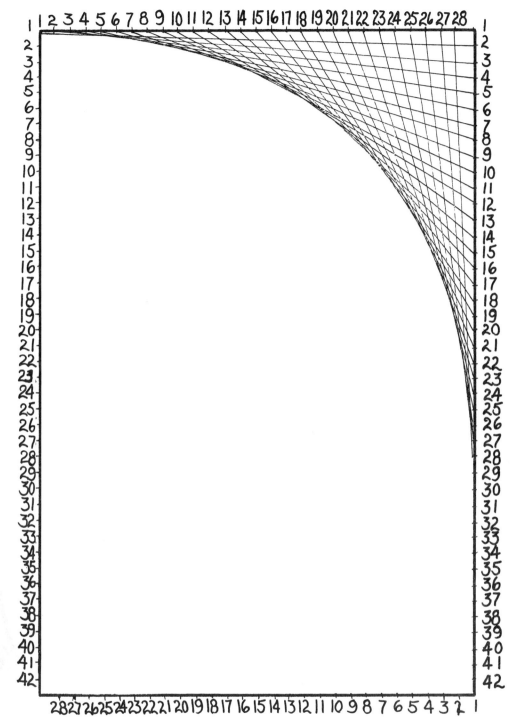

Figure 31   Rectangular Spy threading, step 2.

2.   Now, using Figure 31 as a guide, thread the top and right lines of rectangle A. Tie your thread at brad 1 on the top line and string to brad 2 on the right line and work as follows: 2-2; 2-3; 3-3; and so on.

Repeat these steps to thread rectangles B and C. When threading rectangle D, you use the same one-to-one correspondence method; however, you work step 1 from the right line to the bottom line and you work step 2 from the top line to the left line.

The Rectangular Spy shown here in the color section was worked with the following color scheme:

        Rectangle A: step 1, blue; step 2, dark orange

        Rectangle B: step 1, light orange, step 2, yellow

        Rectangle C: step 1, light purple; step 2, dark purple

        Rectangle D: step 1, blue; step 2, red

This overall design can be threaded in any method you wish. One of the many alternate threading patterns is shown in Figure 32.

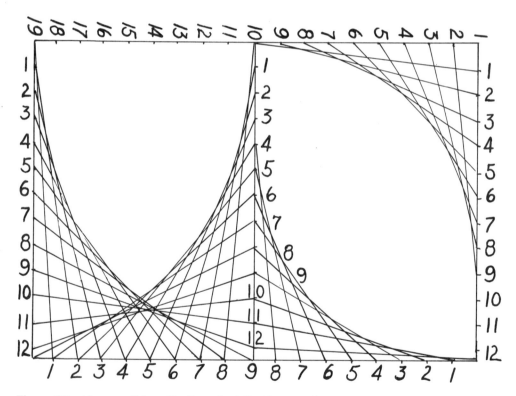

Figure 32   Alternate "threading" method for Rectangular Spy. Starting the threading at any point can change the total effect. Compare right and left side pattern threading.

Six-Pointed Star

This design is made up of two large triangles, 12¾″ on each side, which intersect to form the Six-Pointed Star. When properly de-

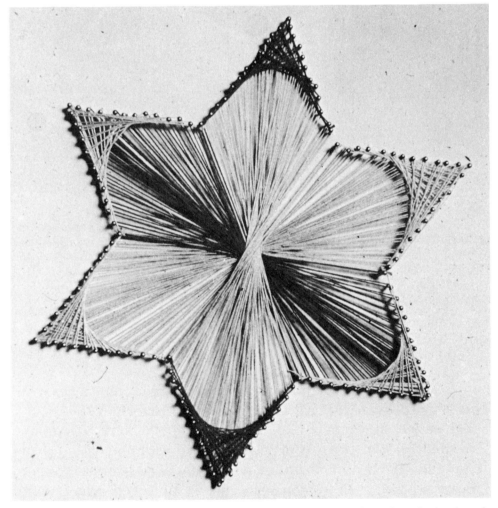

Figure 33a   This Six-Pointed Star is threaded according to instructions given; lattice threading is used on the internal hexagon.

Figure 33b Here is a totally different threading method for the Six-Pointed Star. *Alternate* thread pattern of the Six-Pointed Star is to treat each point as a matching segment of the figure and have all threads crossing in the center. Match all points on one triangle with all points of another: triangle 1 with triangle 4; triangle 2 with triangle 5; triangle 3 with triangle 6. This thread pattern has a second layer in each pointed tip. This is a one-to-one correspondence method in an angular form. This thread pattern is more effective in a monochromatic scheme.

signed, you will have six equilateral triangles surrounding a hexagon. This pattern can be threaded in various ways (see Fig. 33).

The project shown here (Fig. 33a) is threaded with the one-to-one correspondence method. It may be threaded with one or two colors or with an effective monochromatic scheme. The project in Figure 33b was worked with gold metallic thread on a red velvet board, 16″ × 24″.

Making Your Design Pattern

Using Figure 34 as a guide, draw one 12¾″ equilateral triangle. With a ruler measure 4¼″ down each side from the three points and with a pencil mark points A, B, C, D, E, and F. These points will be joined to form the second equilateral triangle: join points A and B, extending the line to 12¾″; join C and D; join E and F.

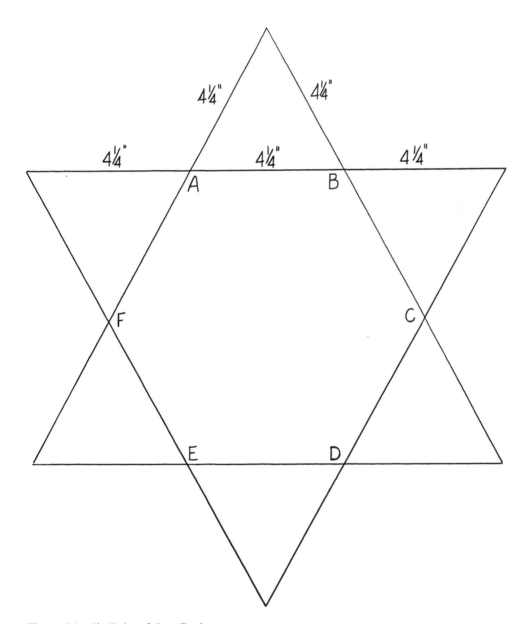

Figure 34   Six-Pointed Star Design pattern.

You should now have two equilateral triangles in proper position for threading.

Working the Threading Pattern

Using Figure 35 as a guide, thread line A with line C as follows: 1-1, 1-2, 2-2, 2-3, and so on. Then thread line B with line C: 1-15, 15-2, 2-14, 14-3, and so on. Work all six triangles the same. Where the two threading patterns overlap, you will have a lattice effect.

The threading pattern used here for the hexagon is also a one-to-one correspondence method with a lattice effect and is worked the same (see Fig. 36) as the six triangles.

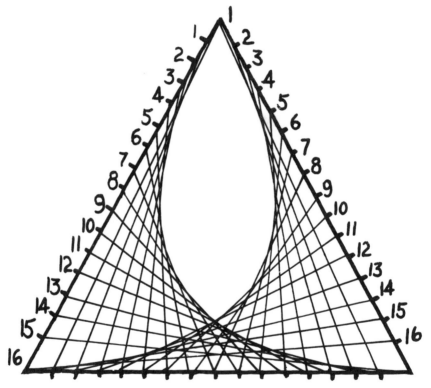

Figure 35   The one-to-one correspondence threading pattern for small triangles.

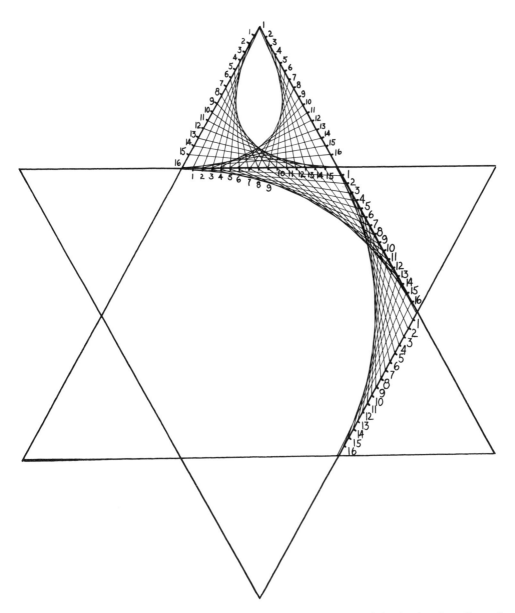

Figure 36 Six-Pointed Star threading pattern for star points and for lattice threading of internal hexagon.

Fish

The fish is a design of excellent geometric form and natural beauty. The variety of species and colors gives you a full range for experimentation in color selection of background fabric and threads.

The design shown in the color section was worked on a gray wool background and the first was threaded with yellow monofilament and the second with light blue monofilament.

The board used here is rectangular (12″ × 24″) but this design can be worked on a larger board with several fish in various positions.

Making Your Design Pattern

To work this design as shown in the color section, you must enlarge the design pattern given in Figure 37.

Trace the pattern onto ½″ graph paper. Now, working line for line, square for square, transfer the design to 1″ graph paper. Your pattern should now be full-size, approximately 10″ at the highest point and 11½″ at the widest point.

All brads should be placed about ¼″ apart and should be labeled as in Figures 38 to 41.

Working the Threading Pattern

1. Using Figure 38 as a guide, triangles A, B, and C are threaded for the fish tail. The threading for each triangle is started at the center brad and is worked in a one-to-one correspondence method with a doubling effect.

Note that triangles A and C have more brads on the diagonal side than on the vertical sides, and triangle B has more brads on the vertical side than the horizontal side. Therefore, when stringing the triangles there is some overlapping of threads known as the *doubling effect*.

40

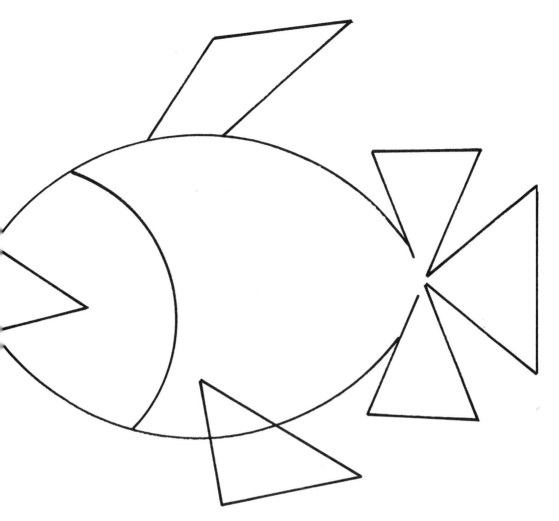

Figure 37   Fish design pattern.

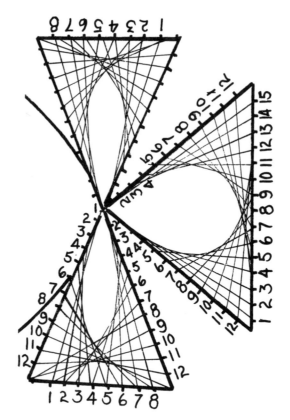

Figure 38   Triangular threading pattern for tail.

For triangles A and C, tie your thread at center brad 1 and pull to brad 1 on the horizontal line. Now, work one diagonal side and then the other side: 1-2; 2-2; 2-3; 3-3; 3-4; 4-4; 4-5; 5-5; 5-6; 6-6; 6-7; 7-7; 7-8; 8-8; 8-9; 9-7; 7-10; 10-6; 6-11; 11-5; 5-12. Tie off.

For triangle B, tie your thread at center brad 1 and pull to brad 1 on the vertical line. Now, work one diagonal side and then the other side: 1-2; 2-2; 2-3; 3-3 . . . 12-12; 12-11; 11-13; 13-10; 10-14; 14-9; 9-15.

2.   Thread the upper and lower fin sections using Figure 39 as a guide. The lower fin is worked in a one-to-one correspondence method, threading the diagonal side with the vertical side and the vertical side with the horizontal side.

The upper fin is a diagonal threading pattern which you can start at any point or work as in Figure 39: thread the brads on the top and bottom lines in a zigzag pattern (see Fig. 14). Next, thread the brads on the top and right lines in an overlapping zigzag pattern.

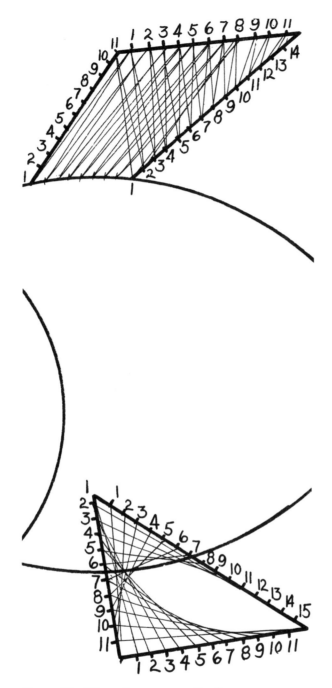

Figure 39   Threading patterns for fins.

43

3.   The head of the fish is strung from the number 1 at the top of the head section to the number 1 brad in the top inner mouth opening (see Fig. 40), loop around brad and return to number 2 brad on the body section, loop around and return to number 2 on the mouth and follow this sequence: 2-3; 3-3; 3-4; 4-4; 4-5; 5-5; 5-6; 6-6; 6-7; 7-7; 7-8; 8-8; 8-9; 9-9; 9-10; 10-10; 10-11; 11-1; 1-11; 11-2; 2-12; 12-3; 3-13; 13-4; 4-14; 14-5; 5-15; 15-6; 6-16; 16-7; 7-18; 18-8. Tie off.

Tie again at brad 12 on the body of the fish (see Fig. 41) and pull thread to brad 27, on the outer bottom mouth and follow this sequence: 27-13; 13-14; 14-14; 14-13; 13-15; 15-12; 12-16; 16-11; 11-17; 17-10; 10-18; 18-9; 9-19; 19-8; 8-20; 20-7; 7-21; 21-6; 6-22; 22-5; 5-23; 23-4; 4-24; 24-3; 3-25; 25-2; 2-26; 26-1; 1-27; 27-8 on the inner bottom mouth opening; 8-14; 14-7; 7-13; 13-6; 6-12; 12-5; 5-11; 11-4; 4-10; 10-3; 3-9; 9-2; 2-8; 8-1 at the inner mouth opening. Tie off.

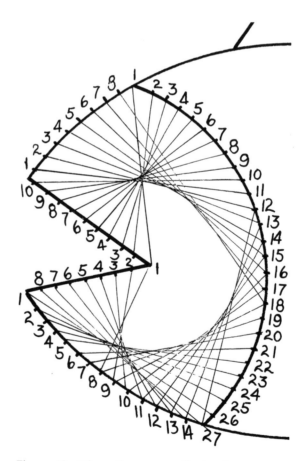

Figure 40   Threading pattern for head.

4.   Using Figure 41 as a guide, work the threading for the bottom of the body section. Tie your thread at brad 9 on the gill section and pull thread to brad 11 on the bottom section of the fish, loop around and return to brad 10, loop around and return to brad 12, and follow this sequence: 12-11; 11-13; 13-12; 12-14; 14-13; 13-15; 15-14; 14-16; 16-15; 15-17; 17-16; 16-18; 18-17; 17-19; 19-18; 18-20; 20-19; 19-21; 21-20; 20-22; 22-21; 21-23; 23-22; 22-24; 24-23; 23-25; 25-24; 24-26; 26-25; 25-X; X-26; 26-X; X-27; 27-X.

5.   Now, work the threading for the top of the body section. For the first layer, follow this sequence. Tie your thread at brad 33 on the tail; pull to brad 1 at the top of the head section; loop around and return to 32 on the tail; 32-2(Y); 2(Y)-31; 31-3; 3-30; 30-4; 4-29; 29-5; 5-28; 28-6; 6-27; 27-7; 7-26; 26-8; 8-25; 25-9; 9-24; 24-10;

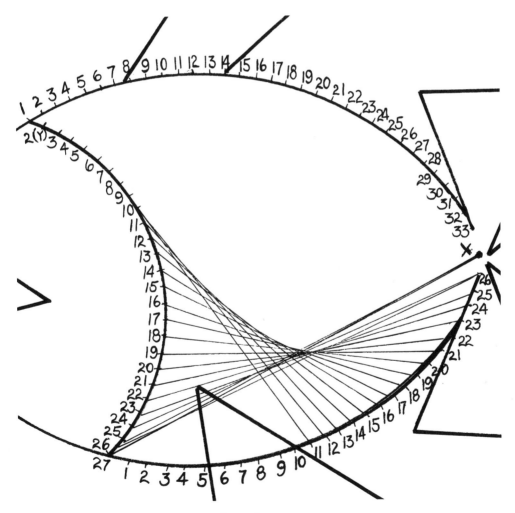

Figure 41   Threading pattern for body section.

10-23; 23-11; 11-22; 22-12; 12-21; 21-13; 13-20; 20-14; 14-19; 19-15; 15-18; 18-16; 16-17; 17-17; 17-16; 16-18; 18-15; 15-19; 19-14; 14-20; 20-13; 13-21; 21-12; 12-22; 22-11; 11-23; 23-10; 10-24; 24-9; 9-25; 25-8; 8-26; 26-7; 7-27. Tie off.

For the second layer, follow this sequence. Tie your thread at brad X; pull tight to brad 1 on the top section of the head; 1-33; 33-2; 2-32; 32-3; 3-31 . . . work this sequence across the top section and down the gill section until 8-27; now work a doubling effect; 27-7; 7-26; 26-6; 6-25; 25-5; 5-24; 24-4; 4-23; 23-3; 3-22; 22-2; 2-21; 21-1. Tie off.

Hexagon

The hexagon pattern is a natural formation found in snowflakes, honeycombs, and tortoise shells. The hexagon used for this project has six sides of equal length, approximately 8″.

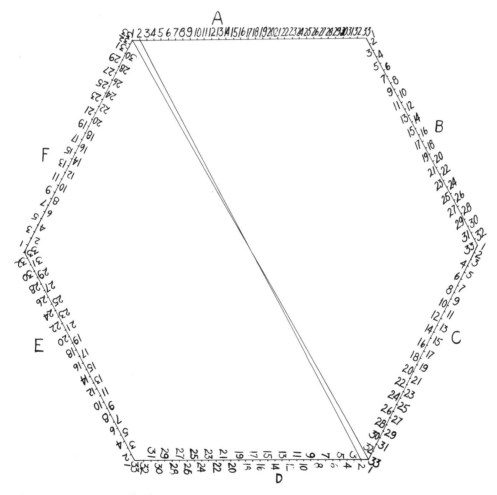

Figure 42   Hexagon Design pattern.

This design works well on a square board; the one used here is 24″ × 24″. The Hexagon Design shown in the color section was worked on beige burlap with yellow, brown, and apricot colored polyester threads.

The hexagon can be used to achieve many interesting effects by changing threading patterns, by working with various types and colors of threads, and by altering the direction of the design on different size or shape boards.

Making Your Design Pattern

Using Figure 42, trace the design onto ¼″ graph paper. Transfer the design line by line, square by square onto 1″ graph paper. Now, your design pattern should be full size, approximately 14¼″ at the highest point and 15¾″ at the widest point.

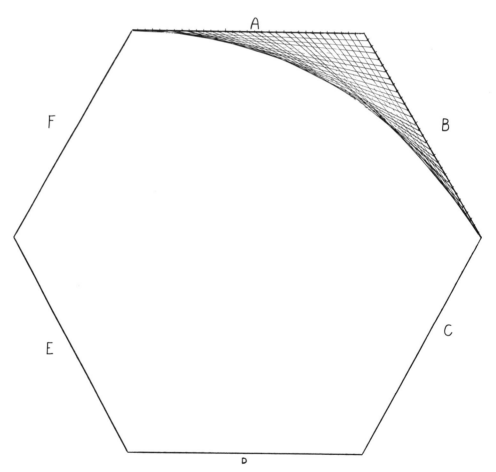

Figure 43   Hexagon Design threading pattern.

All brads should be placed about ¼″ apart. Label your brads according to the numbering in Figure 42.

Working the Threading Pattern

This entire pattern is threaded with the one-to-one correspondence method (see Fig. 43).

1.   Thread side A with side D; side B with side E; side C with side F.

2.   Thread side A with side B; side B with side C; side C with side D; side D with E; side E with side F.

3.   Thread side A with side C; side B with side D; side C with side E; side D with side F; side E with side A.

Each threading step can be worked with a different color thread (see color section).

Hexagon Mosaic

The Hexagon Mosaic Design is a combination of a regular six-sided figure with a diamond in the center; at the top and bottom you have a deltoid or triangular threading pattern.

This design should be worked on a long, horizontal board with good quality fabric and thread. The Hexagon Mosaic shown in the color section was worked on a board 18″ × 36″ on a maroon cotton weave fabric with gold lamé thread.

Since this is a combination of three patterns and each design pattern is worked three times, this project is not recommended as a beginner's project. There are many brads to be hammered and the threading should be exact in every hexagon or else the completed wall hanging will not be uniform.

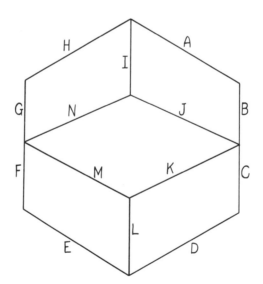

Figure 44 Hexagon Mosaic design with diamond in center and deltoids at top and bottom.

50

Making Your Design Pattern

Using ¼″ graph paper, trace the Hexagon Mosaic design pattern in Figure 44. Now, working line for line and square by square, transfer the design to 1″ graph paper. Your pattern should now be full size, approximately 9¼″ at the widest point and 10¾″ at the highest point.

Working the Threading Pattern

All lines are threaded with the one-to-one correspondence method. Steps 1 to 4 are repeated three times, once for each of the hexagons.

1. First work the inside of the diamond, threading line J with line K and line M with line N with the one-to-one correspondence method (see Fig. 45).

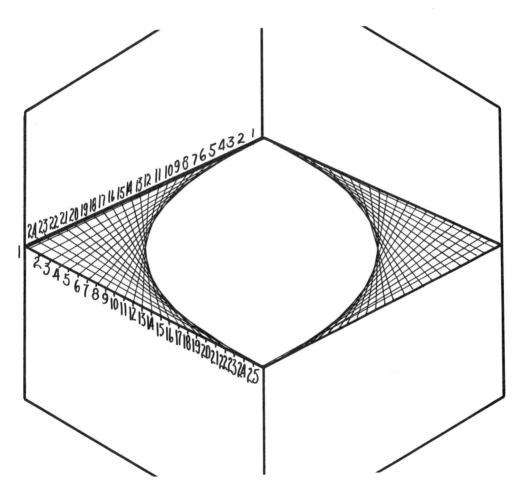

Figure 45   Hexagon Mosaic threading pattern for diamond section.

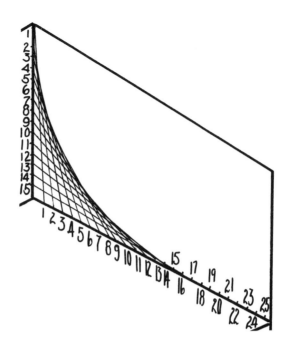

Figure 46　Hexagon Mosaic threading pattern for
the top deltoid section.

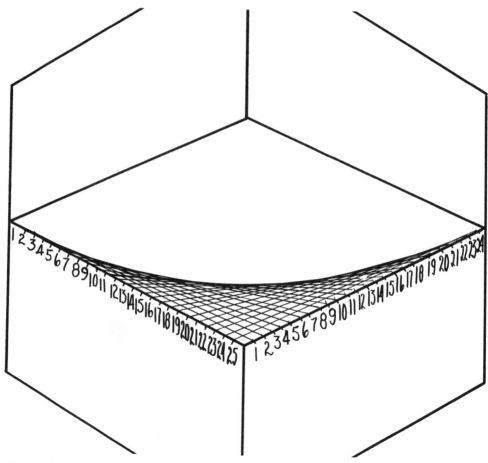

Figure 47　Hexagon Mosaic threading pattern for the deltoid base section.

2. Thread line N with line I; line I with line J; line M with line L; line L with line K (see Fig. 46).

3. Thread line M with line K and line N with line J (see Fig. 47).

4. Now thread line A with line B; line C with line D; line E with line F; and line G with line H (see Fig. 48).

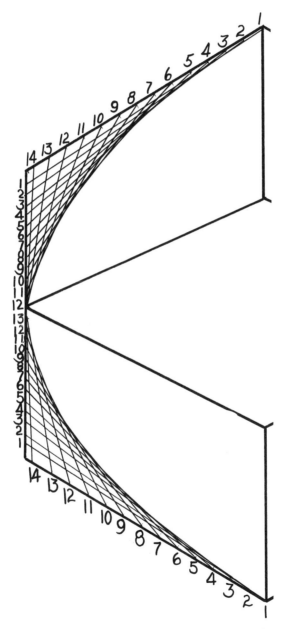

Figure 48   Hexagon Mosaic threading pattern for sides of hexagon.

Solar Flares

This design is a unique composition of arcs and straight lines worked on a black background and strung with a multicolored metallic thread. If you use a polyester or cotton thread, the finished piece will not appear as vibrant as the one shown here in the color section.

The angular rays between the flares are made using brads only; no stringing is called for here.

This design is appropriate for an office or a modern room setting decorated with wood, chrome and glass, or plastic. This design can be used in many ways—on both vertical and horizontal boards. If you plan to use it on a large wall, simply add more Solar Flares to the original design shown here.

The overall dimension of the board used for the project shown in the color section is 16″ × 24″; the overall dimension of the design itself is 14″ × 21″. All brads should be about ¼″ apart.

Making Your Design

Using Figure 49, trace the outline of this full-size pattern for the solar flares; number your brads as shown here. This same pattern is used three times for the overall design. Refer to Figure 50, for proper placement of the three solar flares and for placement and approximate lengths of the angular rays.

To make the project shown here, you will need black felt for the background and variegated (five-color) lamé or metallic crochet thread for the stringing. If you use a polyester or cotton thread, the finished piece will not appear as vibrant as in the project shown here.

Working the Threading Pattern

Note that each arc varies in size and number of points (Fig. 49). Arc A has 23 points; arc B has 26 points; and arc C has 45 points.

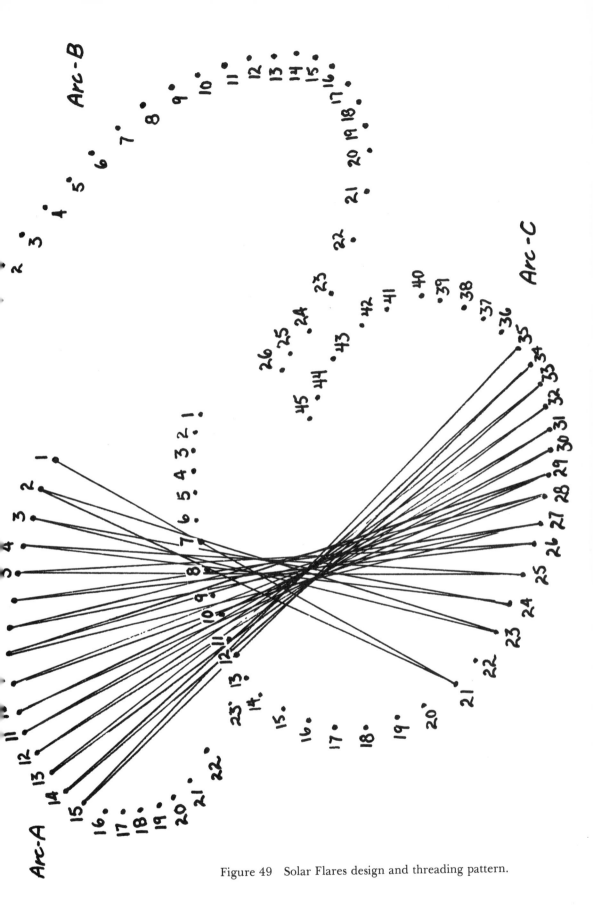

Figure 49   Solar Flares design and threading pattern.

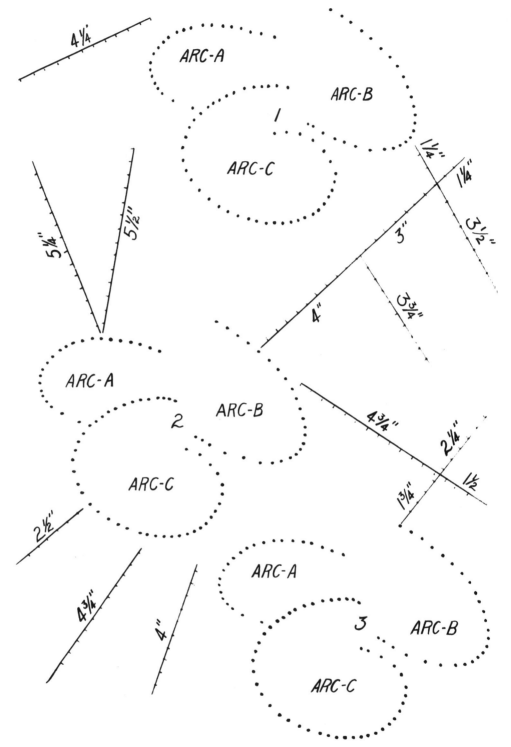

Figure 50   Solar Flares design.

1. For *arcs A and C,* tie the thread at brad 1 on arc A and pull tight to brad 21 on arc C. Loop around and return to brad 2 on arc A; loop around and return to brad 23 on arc C and follow this sequence: 23-3; 3-24; 24-4; 4-25; 25-5; 5-26; 26-6; 6-27; 27-7; 7-28; 28-8; 8-28; 28-9; 9-29; 29-10; 10-30; 30-11; 11-31; 31-12; 12-32; 32-13; 13-33; 33-14; 14-34; 34-15; 15-35; 35-16; 16-36; 36-17; 17-37; 37-18; 18-38; 38-19; 19-39; 39-20; 20-40; 40-21; 21-41; 41-22; 22-42; 42-23; 23-43. Pull thread from number 43 to 13 on arc C; 13 on arc C to 44 on arc C; 44 to 12 on arc C; 12 to 45; 45 on arc C to 11 on arc C, then pull thread to brad 26 on arc B, loop around brad 26 on arc B, pull up to brad 1 on arc C, loop around and return to brad 25 on arc B.

2. Follow this sequence on *arc B*: 25-2; 2-24; 24-3; 3-23; 23-4; 4-22; 22-5; 5-21; 21-6; 6-20; 20-7; 7-19; 19-8; 8-18; 18-9; 9-17; 17-10; 10-16; 16-11; 11-15; 15-12; 12-14; 14-13; 13-15; 15-12; 12-16; 16-11; 11-17; 17-10; 10-18; 18-9; 9-19; 19-8; 8-20; 20-7; 7-21; 21-6; 6-22; 22-5; 5-23; 23-4; 4-22; 22-3; 3-23; 23-2; 2-24; 24-1; 1-25; 25-1; 1-26; 26-1; 1-27; 27-1; 1-23. Tie off.

Work this same threading pattern (Fig. 50) for each solar flare in your design.

Since this a free-form design, you can double your thread or alter the pattern at any point without changing the attractiveness of the pattern.

Note: You can also use this design as clouds; with a blue background and a heavy cotton thread, the result is very pleasing.

Mask

This design is composed of straight lines which form beautiful angles and give the effect of a mask. It can be worked on a vertical or horizontal board.

For the project shown in Figure 51, a black thread was used against a white velour background. This design works best in one color of thread, particularly a cotton crochet thread.

The Mask design can be effectively worked smaller or larger on various size boards; the one used here is 16″ × 24″.

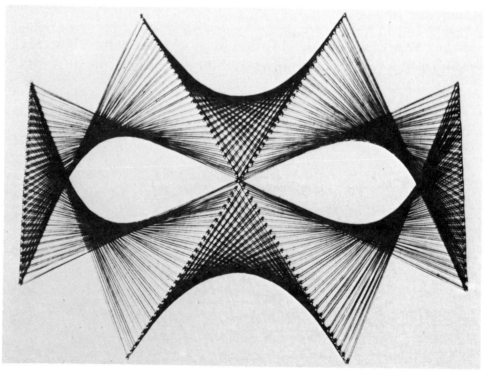

Figure 51   Mask design.

58

Making Your Design Pattern

Using a ruler and pencil and following Figure 52 as a guide, draw your design pattern. Each line (A, B, C, D, E, and F) should be approximately 7" long. The full-size pattern should be about 11½" at the highest point and 14" at the widest point.

Place your brads about ¼" apart. Label the lines A, B, C, D, E, and F; label all brads. Lines B, C, D, and E will have a common center brad (see Fig. 52).

Working the Threading Pattern

All lines are threaded using the one-to-one correspondence method.

1. Thread line A with line B: Tie at brad 1 on line A, pull to brad 1 on line B, return to brad 2 on line A, loop around and return to brad 2 on line B. Follow this sequence: 2-3; 3-3; 3-4; 4-4; 4-5; 5-5; 5-6; 6-6; 6-7; 7-7; 7-8; 8-8; 8-9; 9-9; 9-10; 10-10; 10-11; 11-11; 11-12; 12-12; 12-13; 13-13; 13-14; 14-14; 14-15; 15-15; 15-16; 16-16; 16-17; 17-17; 17-18; 18-18; 18-19; 19-19; 19-20; 20-20; 20-21; 21-21. Tie off.

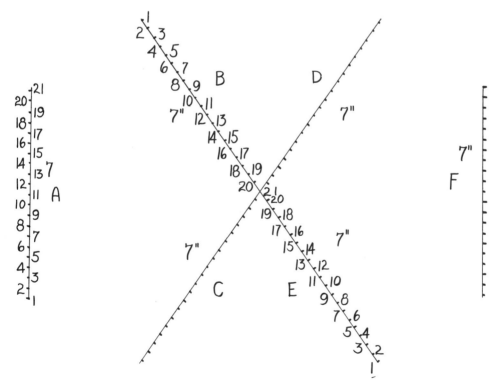

Figure 52   Mask design pattern showing placement of brads.

2.   Thread line A with line C. Brad 21 on line A will become brad 1; brad 20 will become brad 2; numbers are in reverse order and follow the sequence as given above (see Fig. 53).

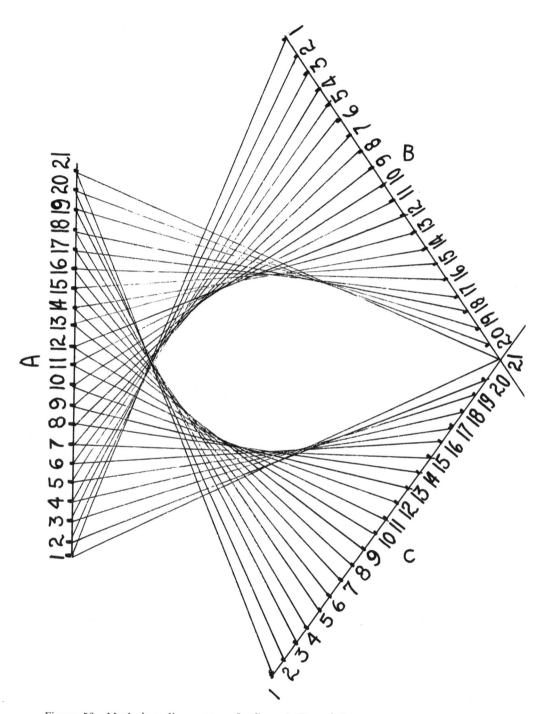

Figure 53   Mask threading pattern for lines A, B, and C.

3. Following the threading sequence given above, thread line B with line D and line C with line E (see Fig. 54).

4. Using this same sequence, thread line F with line D and line F with line E.

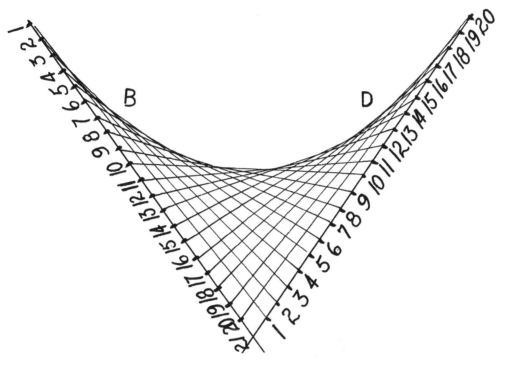

Figure 54 Mask threading pattern for lines B and D.

Ship R.E.S.

The Ship R.E.S. shown in the color section was worked on a black felt background. The white sails are strung with a polyester crochet thread and the ship is strung with metallic silver threads. Galvanized brads are used throughout the design.

The overall dimensions of the board used here are 16″ × 24″; the overall design itself is approximately 10″ × 16″. The brads are ¼″ apart.

Making Your Design Pattern

Using Figure 55, trace the ship pattern onto ½″ tracing paper. Working square by square, transfer the markings to 1″ graph paper. Your pattern should now be full size; the dimensions should correspond with those given in Figure 55.

Insert your brads ¼″ apart and label them according to Figures 56 to 60.

Working The Threading Patterns

1. First you will string *mast 1;* the vertical line has 27 points and the horizontal line has 15 points (see Fig. 56). Tie your thread at brad 1 on the vertical line and pull the thread to brad 1 on the horizontal line. Follow this number sequence: 1-1; 1-2; 2-2; 2-3; 3-3; 3-4; 4-4; 4-5; 5-5; 5-6; 6-6; 6-7; 7-7; 7-8; 8-8; 8-9; 9-9; 9-10; 10-10; 10-11; 11-11; 11-12; 12-12; 12-13; 13-13; 13-14; 14-14; 14-15; 15-15; *do not tie off.*

2. At this point, you must double the horizontal line to complete the vertical line on mast 1. This *doubling effect* is worked as follows: 15-16; 16-14; 14-17; 17-13; 13-18; 18-12; 12-19; 19-11; 11-20; 20-10; 10-21; 21-9; 9-22; 22-8; 8-23; 23-7; 7-24; 24-6; 6-25; 25-5; 5-26; 26-4; 4-27. Tie off.

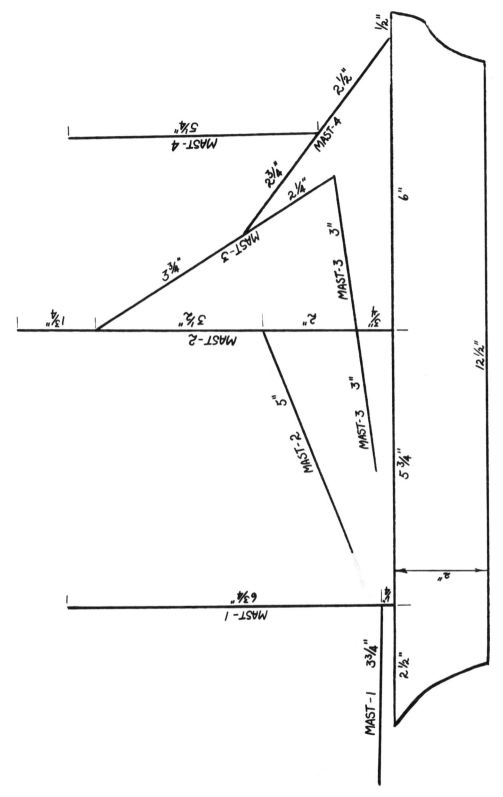

Figure 55 Ship R.E.S. design pattern.

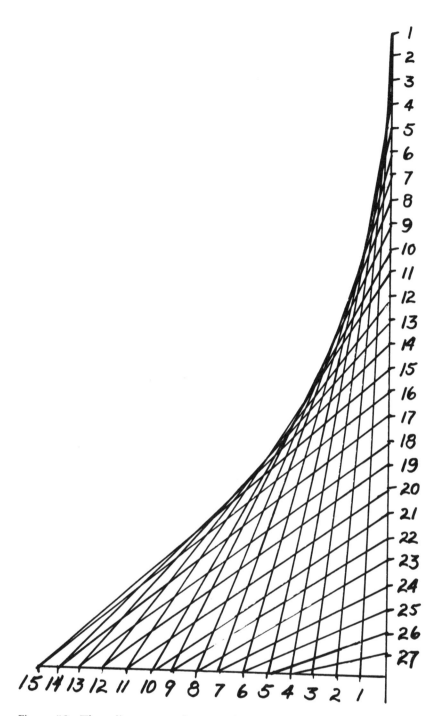

Figure 56   Threading pattern for mast 1.

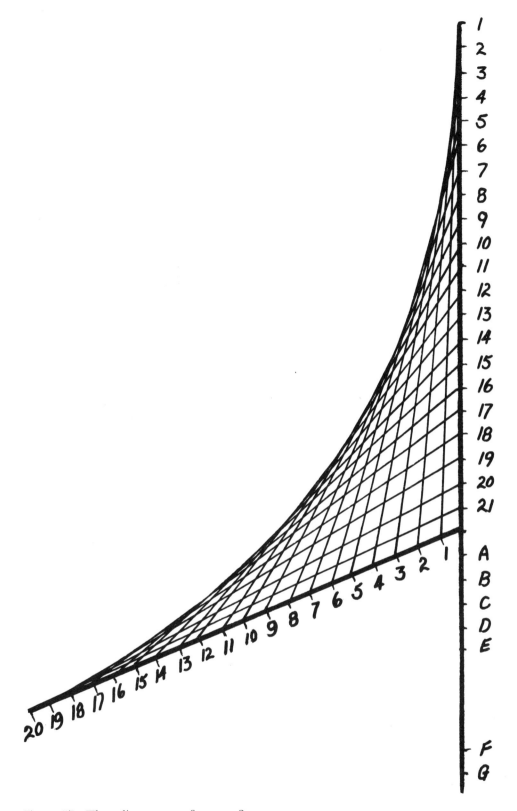

Figure 57   Threading pattern for mast 2.

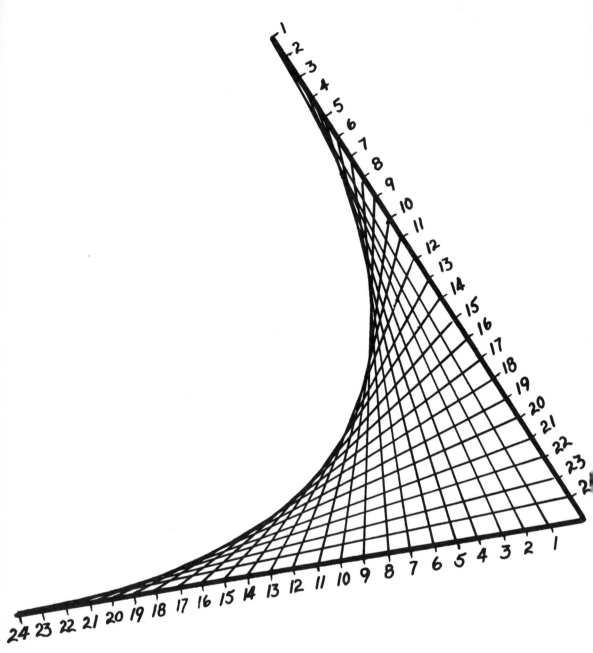

Figure 58   Threading pattern for mast 3.

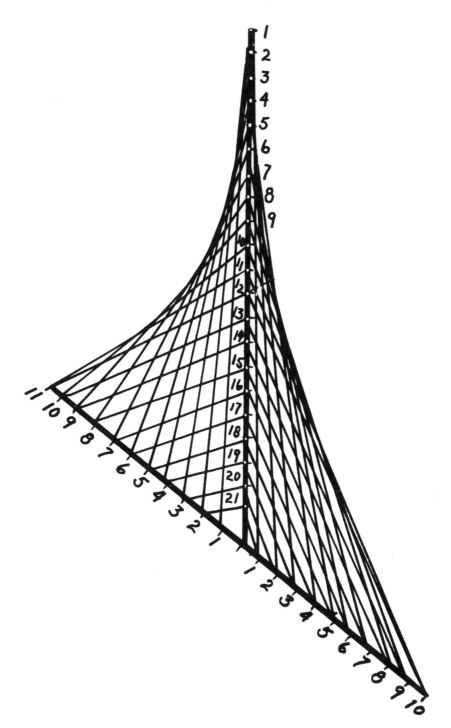

Figure 59   Threading pattern for mast 4.

3.   The threading pattern for *mast 2* is the same as for mast 1. However, the vertical line has 21 points and the horizontal line has 20 points (see Fig. 57). Use the number sequence given in step 1; use the doubling effect to finish the vertical line with its one extra brad.

Note: Leave brads A, B, C, D, E, F, and G free of thread. These form the pole attachment to the ship. The space between brads E and F is the opening for mast 3.

4.   The threading pattern for *mast 3* is a direct one-to-one correspondence method (see Fig. 58) with 24 points on both lines of the angular mast (1-1; 1-2; 2-2; 2-3; . . . 22-23; 23-23; 23-24; 24-24).

5.   The threading pattern for *mast 4* is also a one-to-one correspondence method, but the threading pattern is worked on both sides of the mast pole (see Fig. 59). The right side is numbered 1 to 10; the left side is number 1 to 11. The same doubling technique used on mast 1 must be used here since there are more brads on the vertical line than the other two lines. Observe the diamond-like pattern formed on the doubling thread section.

6.   The threading pattern used for the *body of the ship* is known as the *twisting thread* pattern. The body of the ship is divided into two sections for threading (see Fig. 60 for numbering of brads)—the rear (right side) section and the front (left side) section. Figure 60 shows the twisting thread pattern worked on the *rear section*. This is a one-to-one correspondence method.

7.   Work the *front section* of the body with this same twisting threading pattern. However, it will be necessary to use the doubling technique to complete the threading of the top line of the ship.

Note the numbering on the bottom line of the body: On the rear sections, the numbering is 1 to 24; on the front section, the numbering is 1 to 28. Brad 28 when working the rear section will become brad 24 when working the front section.

8.   Each end of the ship is numbered: front, 1 to 10; rear, 1 to 9. Tie the thread at brad 1 top rear section and pull the thread to brad 28 on the bottom line of the ship. Follow this sequence: 28-2; 2-27; 27-3; 3-26; 26-4; 4-25; 25-5; 5-24; 24-6; 6-23; 23-27; 7-22; 22-8; 8-21; 21-9; 9-21; 21 to brad 1 on the base line. Tie off.

9.   Repeat the above procedure for the front end of the ship, but note the change in the numbering system (1-24; 24-2; 2-23; and so on).

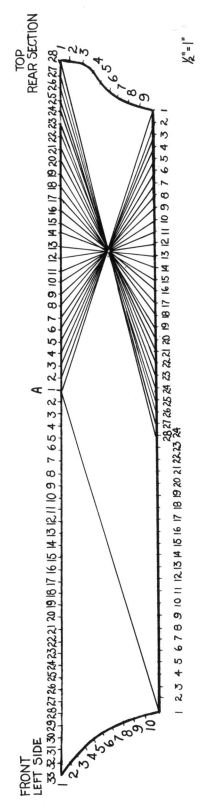

Figure 60   Threading pattern for body of Ship R.E.S.

Fern

This fern design is a practice design for threading curved lines. The stem and bottom spray are simply outlined with brads ¼" apart; the leaves are threaded and joined at the stem, forming V-shaped figures.

This simple curved line design can be used repeatedly to form a border on a long narrow board. It is most attractive when worked in spring-like colors, such as greens, on a rich background fabric. A variety of colors may be used for the leaves. If you choose to work with two colors, first thread the lighter color and then the darker. This Fern design may also be worked in a monochromatic scheme.

The leaves are threaded using the one-to-one correspondence method, forming a twisting pattern in the center of each leaf. The threading may be repeated, starting at any point, or you may leave some of the brads free of thread to highlight the design.

Making Your Design Pattern

Using Figure 61 as a pattern, trace the Fern design onto ½" graph paper. Now transfer the design line by line and square by square onto 1" graph paper. Your pattern should now be full size, approximately 10" at the widest point and 13½" at the highest point.

Place all brads ¼" apart and label them as in Figure 61.

Working the Threading Pattern

Both leaves are threaded with the one-to-one correspondence method.

1. Work leaf A as follows: 1-1; 1-2; 2-2; 2-3; 3-3; 3-4; 4-4; 4-5; 5-5; 5-6; 6-6; 6-7; 7-7; 7-8; 8-8; 8-9; 9-9; 9-10; 10-10; 10-11; 11-12; 12-12; 12-13; 13-13; 13-14; 14-14; 14-15; 15-15. Tie off.

2. Work leaf B as follows: 1-1; 1-2; 2-2; 2-3; 3-3; 3-4; 4-4; 4-5; 5-5; 5-6; 6-6; 6-7; 7-7; 7-8; 8-8; 8-9; 9-9; 9-10; 10-10; 10-11; 11-11; 11-12; 12-12; 12-13; 13-13; 13-14; 14-14; 14-15; 15-15; 15-16; 16-16; 16-17; 17-17; 17-18; 18-18; 18-19; 19-19; 19-20; 20-20. Tie off.

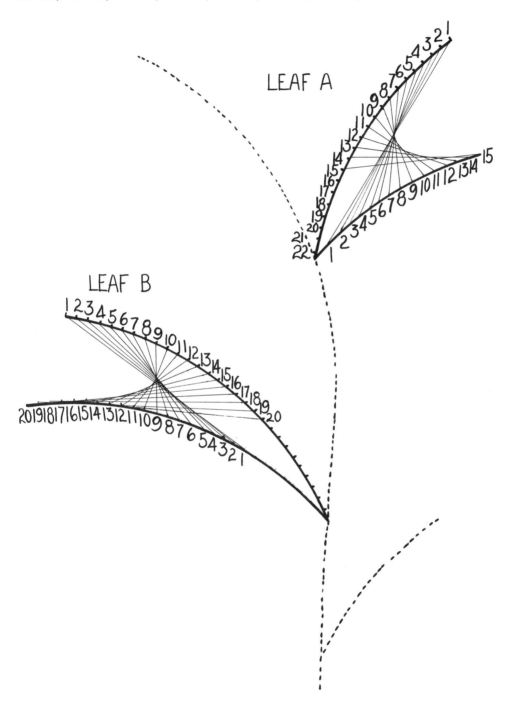

Figure 61   Fern design and threading pattern.

Seashell

There is an abundant supply of ideas for string art in our environment. The water is a great place to look for color and form in its natural state. This Seashell design is a simple curved line that looks much like the famous Chambered Nautilus.

You can make one or more shells on a board in either horizontal or vertical form; or you can use two boards and make one shell on each for a pair of matched wall hangings. The overall dimensions of the board used for this project as shown in the color section are 16″ × 24″; the overall size of the design itself is 8″ × 9½″.

The selection of background fabric is very important in this design. If the finished project is to be placed in a more formal decorative setting such as a living room or bedroom, then a rich quality of fabric, velvet or velour, should be used. The project pictured in the color section was worked on a royal blue velvet background with pink polyester thread.

If placed in a den or recreation room, then you might want to consider a more textural fabric like the weaves, burlaps, or heavy cottons.

Your thread must also blend with your background fabric. If a softer background fabric is used, then you should use a fine polyester or silk thread. If you use a textured fabric, then you should use a cotton thread or crochet yarn. One spool of 225 yards will be sufficient for several threadings of this design.

Making Your Design Pattern

To enlarge this pattern, trace the outline of the design in Figure 62 onto ½″ graph paper. Now, working square by square, transfer the design from the ½″ graph paper to 1″ graph paper. Number the brad points 1 to 52 as shown; the brads should all be ½″ apart. Your

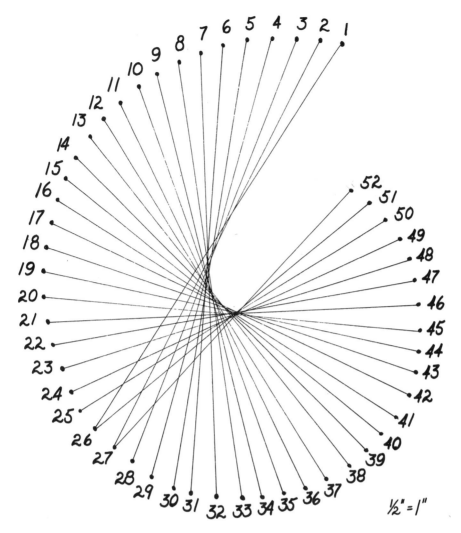

½″ = 1″

Figure 62   Seashell design and threading pattern.

pattern should now be full size, approximately 9½″ at the highest point and 8″ at the widest. It is now ready to be used.

Working the Threading Pattern

Tie thread to brad 1 and pull tight to brad 26; follow this sequence: 26-2; 2-27; 27-3; 3-28; 28-4; 4-29; 29-5; 5-30; 30-6; 6-31; 31-7; 7-32; 32-8; 8-33; 33-9; 9-34; 34-10; 10-35; 35-11; 11-36; 36-12; 12-37; 37-13; 13-38; 38-14; 14-39; 39-15; 15-40; 40-16; 16-41; 41-17; 17-42; 42-18; 18-43; 43-19; 19-44; 44-20; 20-45; 45-21; 21-46; 46-22; 22-47; 47-23; 23-48; 48-24; 24-49; 49-25; 25-50; 50-26; 26-51; 51-27; 27-52. Tie off.

73

This threading pattern should be repeated at least twice if you are using a fine thread as in the project shown on the cover. However, if a heavy cotton thread has been used, then one threading is probably sufficient.

You may repeat the pattern as many times as you want to achieve the look you want. Experiment to satisfy your tastes.

Football Helmet

The Football Helmet design shown in Figure 63 was worked on a 16″ × 24″ board with a white felt background and black cotton crochet thread. Why not work this design in your team's favorite colors?

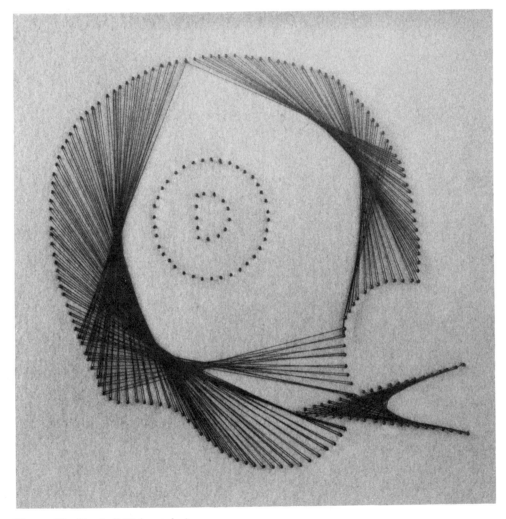

Figure 63   Football Helmet design.

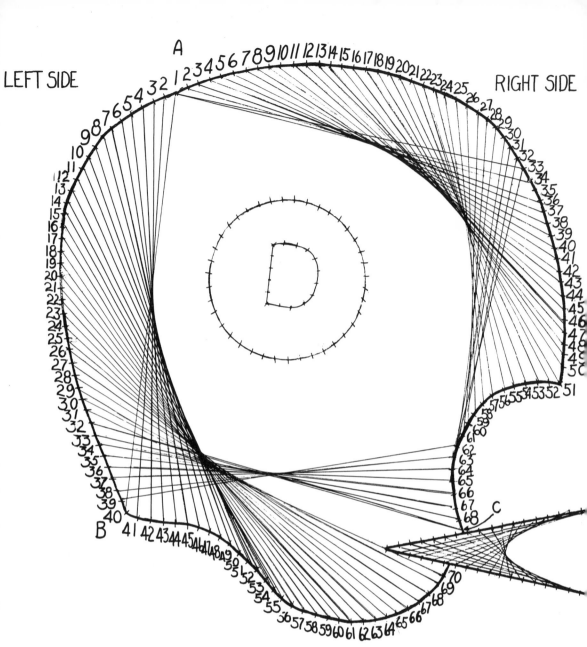

Figure 64   Football Helmet threading pattern.

Making Your Design Pattern

Using Figure 64, trace the design onto ½" graph paper. Working line by line and square by square, transfer the design to 1" graph paper. Your pattern should now be full size, approximately 11½" at the highest point and 10¾" at the widest point.

Insert all brads about ¼" apart and label them as in Figure 64. Note that the brads on the left side of the helmet are numbered 1 to 70; on the right side, they are numbered 1 to 69. The guard section (Fig. 65) has 21 brads on the top section and 19 brads on the bottom. Also, label points A, B, and C.

Working the Threading Pattern

The circle and the team initial are left open, without threading.

1. Starting at point A (see Fig. 64), thread the left side, following this sequence: Tie thread at brad 1, pull to brad 40, point B at the base; return to brad 2; 2-41; 41-3; 3-42; 42-4; 4-43; 43-5; 5-44; 44-6; 6-45; 45-7; 7-46; 46-8; 8-47; 47-9; 9-48; 48-10; 10-49; 49-11; 11-50; 50-12; 12-51; 51-13; 13-52; 52-14; 14-53; 53-15; 15-54; 54-16; 16-55; 55-17; 17-56; 56-18; 18-57; 57-19; 19-58; 58-20; 20-59; 59-21; 21-60; 60-22; 22-61; 61-23; 23-62; 62-24; 24-63; 63-25; 25-64; 64-26; 26-65; 65-27; 27-66; 66-28; 28-67; 67-29; 29-68; 68-30; 30-69; 69-31; 31-70. Tie off.

2. Starting again at point A (see Fig. 64), thread the right side as follows: Tie at brad 1, pull to brad 33, return to brad 2; 2-34; 34-3; 3-35; 35-4; 4-36; 36-5; 5-37; 37-6; 6-38; 38-7; 7-39; 39-8; 8-40; 40-9; 9-41; 41-10; 10-42; 42-11; 11-43; 43-12; 12-44; 44-13; 13-45; 45-14; 14-46; 46-15; 15-47; 47-16; 16-48; 48-17; 17-49; 49-18; 18-50; 50-19; 19-51; 51-20; 20-52; 52-21; 21-53; 53-22; 22-54; 54-23; 23-55; 55-24; 24-56; 56-25; 25-57; 57-26; 26-58; 58-27; 27-59; 59-28; 28-60; 60-29; 29-61; 61-30; 30-61. Tie off.

3. Starting at point C (see Fig. 64), work the threading to complete the top and frontal sections of the helmet: Tie your thread at brad 69, point C; pull across to brad 32; 32-68; 68-33; 33-67; 67-34; 34-66; 66-35; 35-65; 65-36; 36-64; 64-37; 37-63; 63-38; 38-62; 62-39. Tie off.

If you wish to have heavier lines, you may repeat the threading process at least twice, or you may change to a thicker yarn (wool or cotton) for the threading.

4. The guard section (see Fig. 65) is worked in the one-to-one

correspondence method: Tie your thread at top brad 1; pull to bottom brad 19; return to top brad 2; 2-18; 18-3; 3-17; 17-4; 4-16; 16-5; 5-15; 15-6; 6-14; 14-7; 7-13; 13-8; 8-12; 12-9; 9-11; 11-10; 10-10; 10-11; 11-9; 9-12; 12-8; 8-13; 13-7; 7-14; 14-6; 6-15; 15-5; 5-16; 16-4; 4-17; 17-3; 3-18; 18-2; 2-19; 19-1; 1-20; 20-2; 2-21. Tie off.

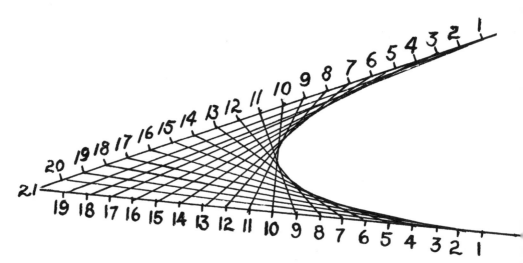

Figure 65   Football Helmet threading pattern for guard section.

Web

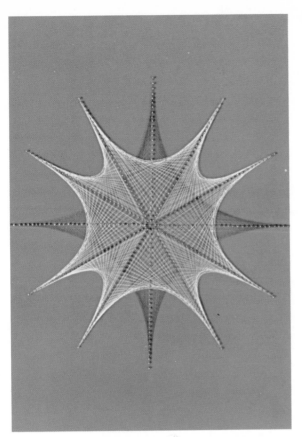

Rectangular Spy

Fish

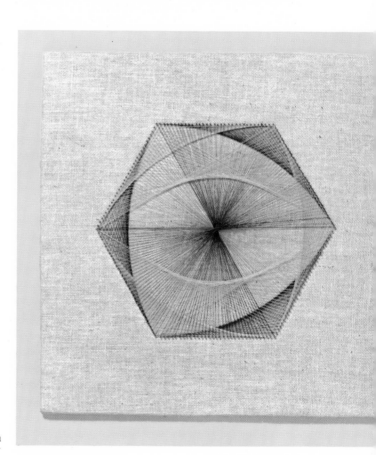

Hexagon Design

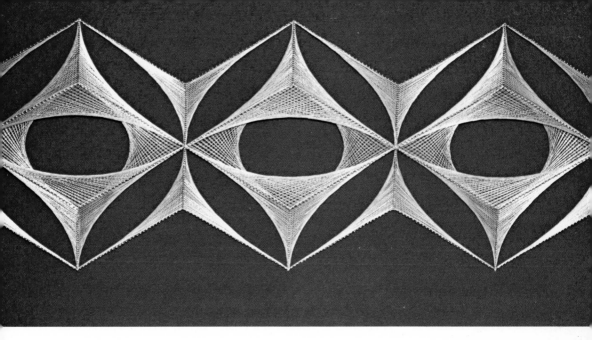

Hexagon Mosaic

Solar Flares
(Photo by Bruce V. Miller)

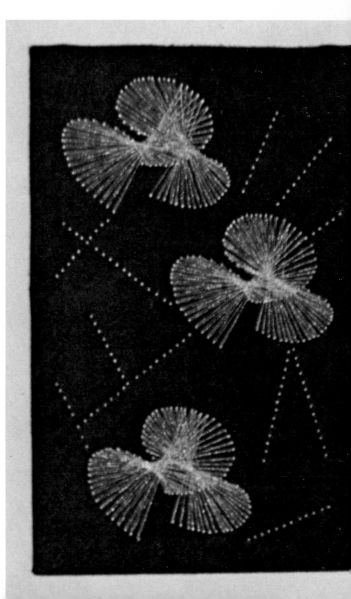

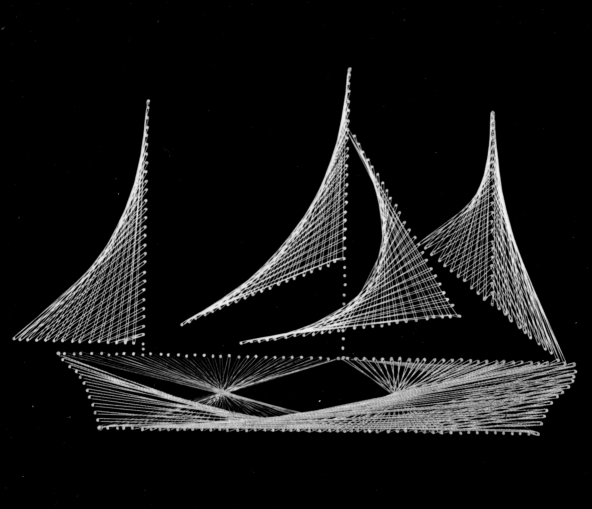

Ship R.E.S.

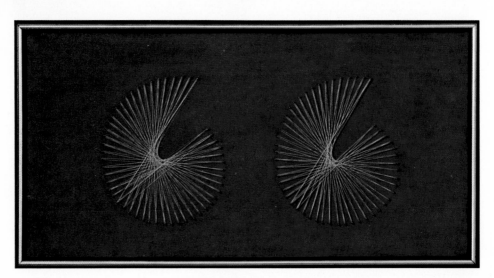

Seashells

Astro-Copter

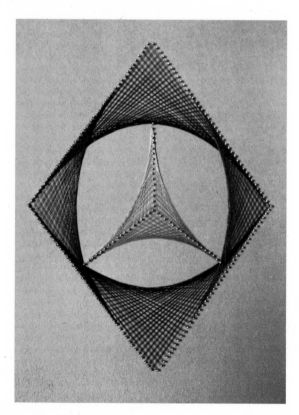

Diamond Deltoid

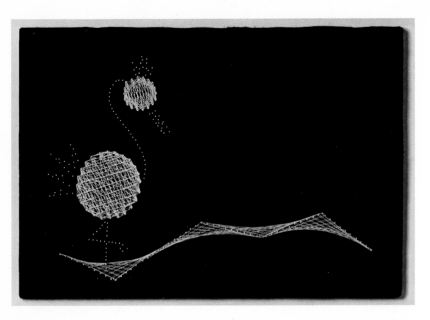

Flamingo
(Photo by Bruce V. Miller)

Sharpie the Cruiser

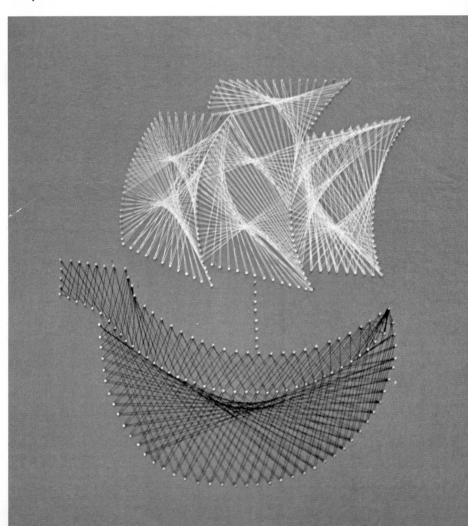

Panda
(Photo by Bruce V. Miller)

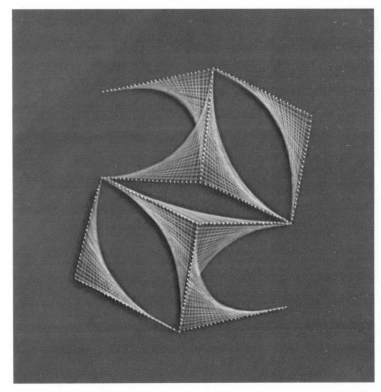

Quadrilateral Composition

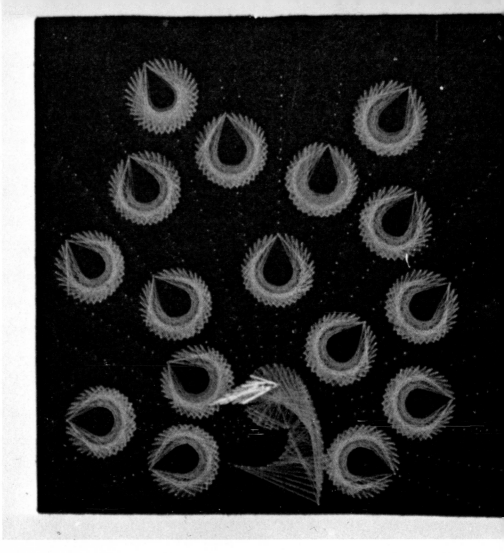

Peacock
(Photo by Bruce V. Miller)

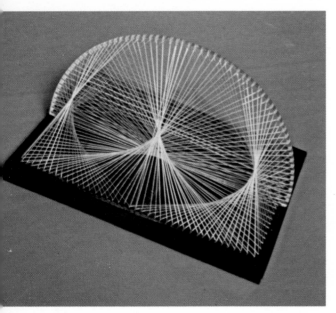

Three-Dimensional Desk Accent Piece

Astro-Copter

The Astro-Copter design (see color section) is a combination of straight lines and circles. This design is most effective on a vertical board with a dark background fabric and metallic or silk thread.

The Astro-Copter in the color section was worked on a 16″ × 24″ board with gold metallic thread on a dark orange felt background fabric.

Making Your Design Pattern

The top (Astro) section of this design has two lines divided into four equal line segments, A, B, C, and D. These lines should be proportionate to the background board dimensions. Each segment should be no longer than 4″ if the design is worked on a 16″ × 24″ board.

Using Figure 66 as a guide, trace the top section and extend lines A, B, C, and D to 4″ each. Place all brads ¼″ apart and label them 1 to 16 as in Figure 66.

The bottom (Copter or blade) section has two concentric circles. Using Figure 67 as a guide, trace the design circles and mark all brad points. Each circle is divided into 36 points. The outer circle should have a diameter of 6″ and the inner circle 4″.

The brad used at the center point A should be at least 1½″ high, since all threading on the circles is worked to and from this center point.

Working the Threading Pattern

1.   The top section of the Astro-Copter is threaded with the one-to-one correspondence method. Thread line A with line B, following this sequence: 1-1; 1-2; 2-2; 2-3; 3-3; 3-4; 4-4; 4-5; 5-5; 5-6; 6-6; 6-7;

79

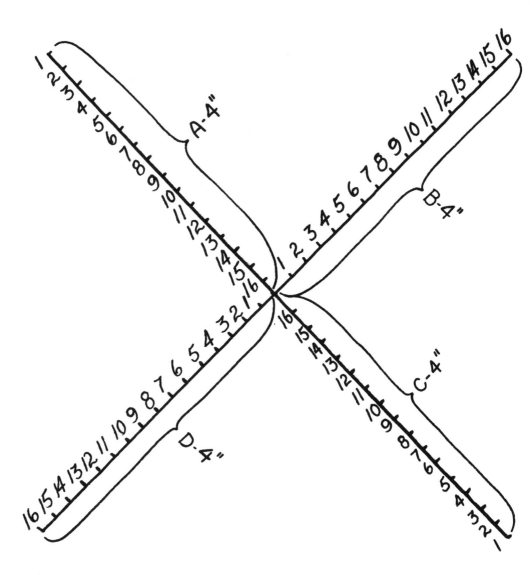

Figure 66   Pattern for the (Astro) top section of the Astro-Copter design.

7-7; 7-8; 8-8; 8-9; 9-9; 9-10; 10-10; 10-11; 11-11; 11-12; 12-12; 12-13; 13-13; 13-14; 14-14; 14-15; 15-15; 15-16; 16-16. Tie off.

2.   Now, using this same threading pattern, work line B with line C; line C with line D; and line D with line A.

3.   The threading for the concentric circles is worked from the center brad A, following this sequence: Tie your thread at brad A; loop around and pull tight to brad 1: loop around and return to brad A; A-2; 2-A; A-3; 3-A; A-4; 4-A; A-5; 5-A . . . 71-A; A-72; 72-A. Tie off. Work this pattern around all 72 points of the circle section; notice

80

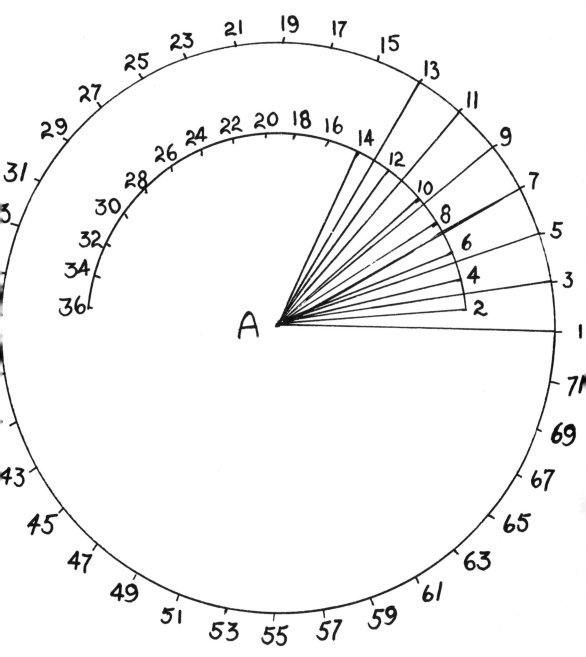

Figure 67   Pattern for the bottom (Copter) section of the Astro-Copter design.

that throughout this threading pattern you will have two threads running from each brad to the center.

4.   To attach the Astro section to the Copter, tie the thread at brad 1 on line C and pull tight to center brad A in the circle; loop around and return to brad 1 on C. Tie off.

Double Daisy

The Double Daisy design is a composition of straight lines for the stem and leaves, a circle for the center of the flower, and heart-like arcs for the petals. ·

This attractive spring flower design will cheer up any room when threaded with lively colors on a rich background. The project shown in Figure 68 was worked on a light green wool fabric with dark green cotton thread for the leaves. The petals were worked in white with a bright yellow center. The stems should be strung in a good contrasting green. The overall dimensions of the background board are 16″ × 24″.

This design can be worked on a horizontal board with three or more daisies. The Fern design (see Fig. 61) can be used for the stem so that the flowers can be worked closer together for a more attractive flower arrangement.

Making Your Design Pattern

With a ruler and pencil and using Figure 69 as a guide, draw the stem and leaves of the daisy.

Using Figure 69, trace the flower onto ½″ graph paper. Now, working line by line and square by square, transfer the design to 1″ graph paper. Your flower pattern should now be full size, approximately 8″ at the highest point and 8¾″ at the widest point. Also, transfer all markings for brad placement.

Working Your Threading Pattern

1. To thread the stem, a diagonal (zigzag) threading pattern is used (see Fig. 14), starting at brad 1 and working down the stem (see Fig. 69). Tie your thread at brad 1 on the right side; pull to brad 1 on the left side; loop around and return to brad 2 on the right; and work

Figure 68   Double Daisy design.

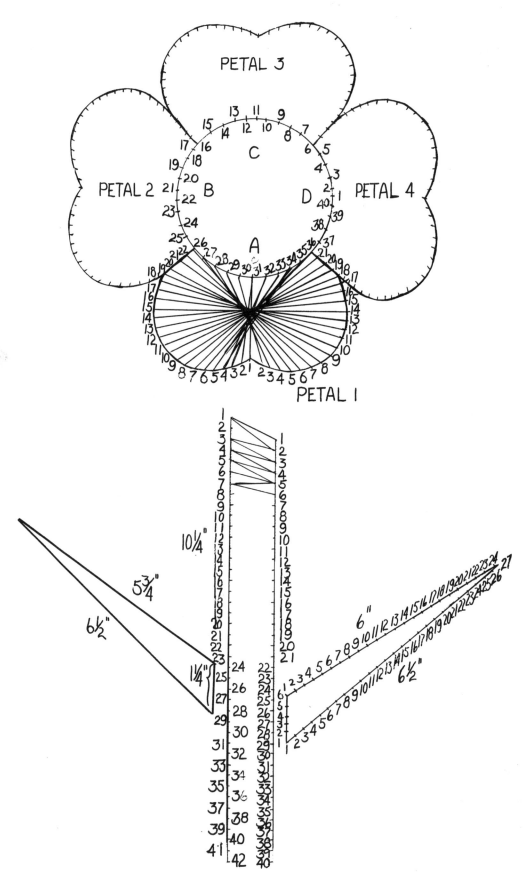

Figure 69 Double Daisy design pattern.

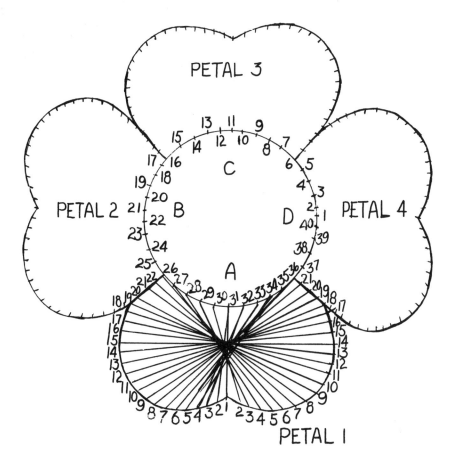

Figure 70   Double Daisy threading pattern.

as follows: 2-3; 3-3; 3-4; 4-4 . . . until completed. This pattern should be repeated at least two or three times for extra depth.

2.   The leaves around the stem may be left free of thread, or you may place brads ¼″ apart and work the diagonal (see Fig. 14) or lattice (see Fig. 13b) threading pattern as shown in Figure 69. Work the leaves as follows: Tie your thread at the edge of leaf brad 27; pull thread to base brad X; loop around and return to brad 26 on the lower side of the leaf; loop around and return to base brad 2: 2-25; 25-3; 3-24; 24-4; 4-23; 23-5; 5-22; 22-1 on the upper side of the leaf; pull thread tight to brad 27 at the point of the leaf. Tie off.

The brads on the upper side have been omitted in the completed design shown in Figure 68. These brads can be added if there is a desire for a fuller leaf; the diagonal threading pattern can be worked here.

3.   To thread the flower, work petal 1 as follows: Tie your thread

at brad A(31); pull to brad 1; loop around and return to brad A(30); A(30)-2; 2-A(29); A(29)-3; 3-A(28); A(28)-4; 4-A(27); A(27)-5; 5-A(26); A(26)-6; 6-22; 22-7; 7-21; 21-8; 8-20; 20-9; 9-19; 19-10; 10-18; 18-11; 11-17; 17-12; 12-16; 16-13; 13-15; 15-14; 14-14; 14-15; 15-13; 13-16; 16-12; 12-17; 17-11; 11-18; 18-10; 10-19; 19-9; 9-20; 20-8; 8-21; 21-7; 7-A(36); A(36)-6; 6-A(35); A(35)-5; 5-A(34); A(34)-4; 4-A(33); A(33)-3; 3-A(32); A(32)-2; 2-A(31).

4. Starting at brads B(21), C(11), and D(1), thread petals 2, 3, and 4, respectively, using the above sequence. Note that you will move to your left around the circle and to your right on the petal as you work each threading sequence.

5. The center of the circle is threaded as follows: 1-2; 2-40; 40-4; 4-39; 39-5; 5-38; 38-6; 6-37; 37-7; 7-36; 36-8; 8-35; 35-9; 9-34; 34-10; 10-33; 33-11; 11-32; 32-12; 12-31; 31-13; 13-30; 30-14; 14-29; 29-15; 15-28; 28-16; 16-27; 27-17; 17-26; 26-18; 18-25; 25-19; 19-24; 24-20; 20-23; 23-21; 21-22. Tie off. At least three layers of threading should be worked on this center section and then a lattice (padding) effect should be added (see Fig. 13b).

Comet

The Comet is a nebulous body that revolves around the sun and is one of the most fascinating phenomena of the skies.

This design can be worked in a metallic or variegated thread on a wood surface as in the project shown in Figure 71 or on a fabric covered board, 16" × 24". Two or more thread colors may be applied for an interesting effect; red and white thread were alternately used in this design. If worked on a wood background, paint the surface in a flat finish or stain so that the threading will show. You may also use wire, available in several colors, for threading this design.

Since the threading for this design is worked in three layers from brads 1, 2, and 24, these three brads should be at least 1½" in length and must be hammered firmly in position.

Making Your Design Pattern

Using Figure 72, trace the design onto ¼" graph paper. Now, working line by line and square by square, transfer the design to 1" graph paper. Your pattern should now be full size, approximately 14¾" at the highest and widest points; each line should be four times as long as it appears in Figure 72.

Working the Threading Pattern

1. Using Figure 73 as a guide, start the threading as follows: Tie your thread at brad 1; pull thread to brad 3; loop around and return to brad 1; 1-4; 4-1; 1-5; 5-1; 1-6; 6-1; 1-7; 7-1; 1-8; 8-1; 1-9; 9-1; 1-10; 10-1; 1-11; 11-1; 1-12; 12-1; 1-13; 13-1; 1-14; 14-1; 1-15; 15-1; 1-16; 16-1; 1-17; 17-1; 1-18; 18-1; 1-19; 19-1; 1-20; 20-1; 1-21; 21-1; 1-22; 22-1; 1-23; 23-1. Tie off.

2. Now, work the same sequence around the comet, starting at brad 2: 2-4; 4-2; 2-5; 5-2 . . . 2-23; 23-2; 2-24; 24-2. Tie off.

Figure 71   Comet design with five threading layers.

3.   Now, work the same sequence around the comet, starting at brad 24: 24-2; 2-24; 24-3; 3-24 . . . 24-21; 21-24; 24-22; 22-24. Tie off.

The instructions given here are for three threading layers, with each layer starting at a different brad. The project shown in Figure 71 is worked with five layers from five different brads. Each brad on the Comet could be used as a starting brad for additional threading layers.

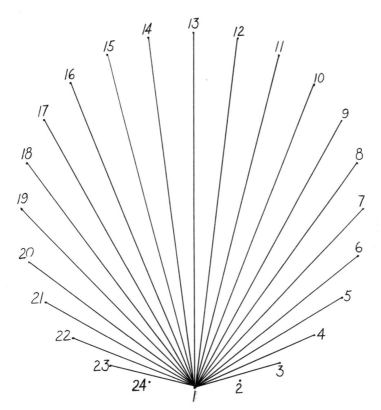

Figure 72   Comet design pattern.

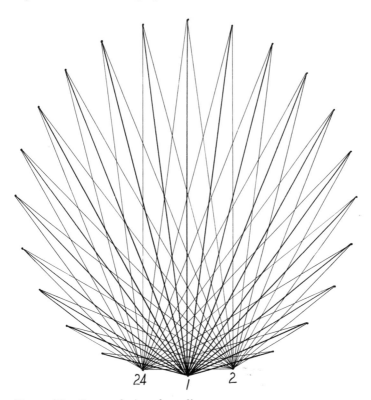

Figure 73   Comet design threading pattern.

Diamond Deltoid

This design is created by combining the diamond and the deltoid. This design can be used in a vertical or horizontal position and is a good design for blending colors.

The project shown in the color section was worked on a 16″ × 24″ board covered with yellow felt and threaded with black for the diamond and burnt orange for the deltoid.

Making Your Design Pattern

Using Figure 74, trace the design onto ½″ graph paper. Now, working line by line and square by square, transfer the design to 1″ graph paper. Your pattern should now be full size, approximately 16″ at the highest point and 12″ at the widest point. Note that the top line of the deltoid (E) is in direct line with the top corner of the diamond, the right line (F) is in direct line with brad 16 on line A, and the left line (G) is in direct line with brad 26 on line B.

Label lines A to G and place all brads (a total of 209) ¼″ apart and label them as in Figure 75.

Working the Threading Pattern

This entire project is worked in the one-to-one correspondence method.

1. Start by threading diamond sides A and B (see Fig. 75) as follows: Tie your thread at brad 1 on side A; pull thread tight to brad 2 on side B; loop around and return to brad 2 on side A; and then follow this sequence: 2-3; 3-3; 3-4; 4-4; 4-5; 5-5; 5-6; 6-6; 6-7; 7-7; 7-8; 8-8; 8-9; 9-9; 9-10; 10-10; 10-11; 11-11; 11-12; 12-12; 12-13; 13-13; 13-14; 14-14; 14-15; 15-15; 15-16; 16-16; 16-17; 17-17; 17-18; 18-19; 19-19; 19-20; 20-20; 20-21; 21-21; 21-22; 22-22; 22-23; 23-24; 24-24; 24-25; 25-25; 25-26; 26-26; 26-27; 27-27; 27-28; 28-28; 28-29;

90

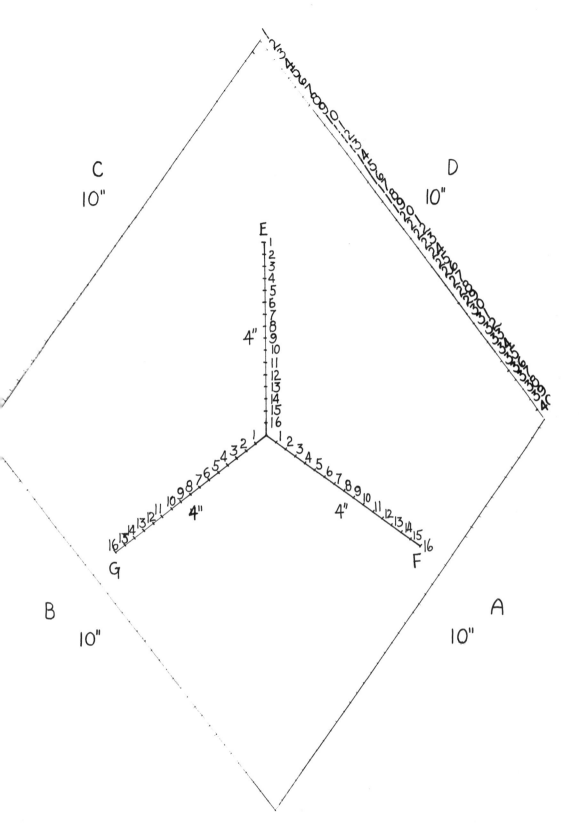

Figure 74 Diamond-Deltoid design pattern.

91

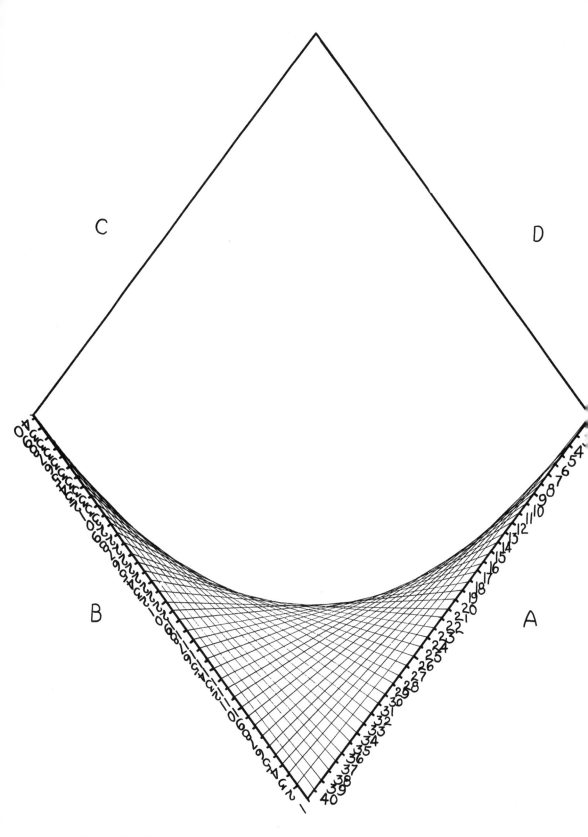

Figure 75   Threading pattern for sides A and B of Diamond.

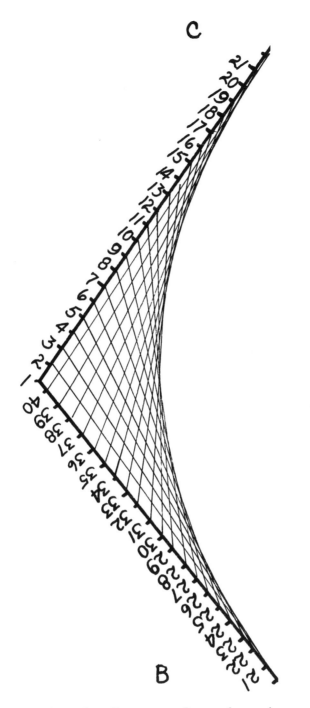

Figure 76   Threading pattern for overlay sections
(sides B and C) within the Diamond.

29-29; 29-30; 30-30; 30-31; 31-31; 31-32; 32-32; 32-33; 33-33; 33-34; 34-34; 34-35; 35-35; 35-36; 36-36; 36-37; 37-37; 37-38; 38-38; 38-39; 39-39; 39-40; 40-40. Tie off.

2.   Now, work sides C and D, using the same threading sequence: Tie your thread at brad 1 on side C; pull the thread tight to brad 2 on side D; loop around and return to brad 2 on side C; and follow the above sequence: 2-3; 3-3; 3-4 . . . 39-40; 40-40. Tie off.

3.   For the small overlay sections within the diamond (see Fig. 76), thread side B with side C as follows: Tie your thread at brad 21 on side B and pull thread tight to brad 2 on side C; 2-22; 22-3; 3-23; 23-4; 4-24; 24-5; 5-25; 25-6; 6-26; 26-7; 7-27; 27-8; 8-28; 28-9; 9-29; 29-10; 10-30; 30-11; 11-31; 31-12; 12-32; 32-13; 13-33; 33-14; 14-34; 34-15; 15-35; 35-16; 16-36; 36-17; 17-37; 37-18; 18-38; 38-19; 19-39; 39-20; 20-40; 40-21; 21-1 on side C. Tie off.

4.   Now, work the second overlay section by threading side D with side A, following the above sequence: Tie your thread at brad 21 on side D and pull tight to brad 2 on side A; 2-22; 22-3; 3-23 . . . 20-40; 40-21; 21-1 on side A. Tie off.

5.   To work the deltoid in the center of the diamond (see Fig. 77), thread line E with line F as follows: Tie your thread at brad 1 on line E and pull to brad 1 on line F; 1-2; 2-2; 2-3; 3-3; 3-4; 4-4; 4-5; 5-5; 5-6; 6-6; 6-7; 7-7; 7-8; 8-8; 8-9; 9-9; 9-10; 10-10; 10-11; 11-11; 11-12; 12-12; 12-13; 13-13; 13-14; 14-14; 14-15; 15-15; 15-16; 16-16. Tie off.

6.   Work this same sequence to thread line E with line G.

7.   Now, thread line G with line F as follows: Tie your thread at brad 1 on line G and pull to brad 16 on line F; 16-2; 2-15; 15-3; 3-14; 14-4; 4-13; 13-5; 5-12; 12-6; 6-11; 11-7; 7-10; 10-8; 8-9; 9-9; 9-8; 8-10; 10-7; 7-11; 11-6; 6-12; 12-5; 5-13; 13-4; 4-14; 14-3; 3-15; 15-2; 2-16; 16-1. Tie off.

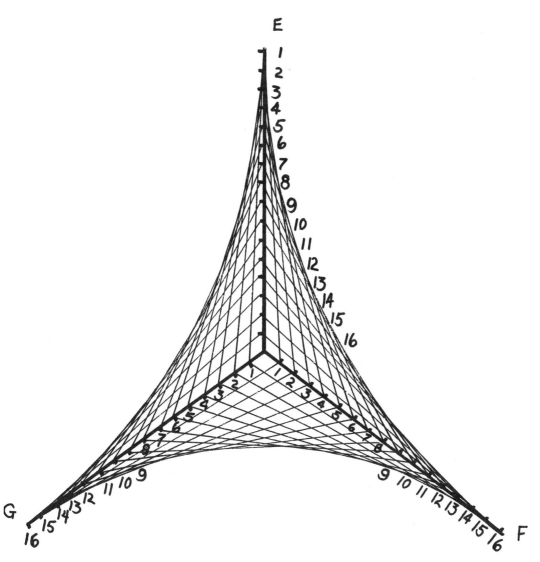

Figure 77   Threading pattern for the Deltoid.

Circle Flower

The circle is one of the most useful design patterns. The overlapping of circles makes an attractive flower or fan-like design. The Circle Flower shown in Figure 78 is made of five 6¾″ diameter overlapping

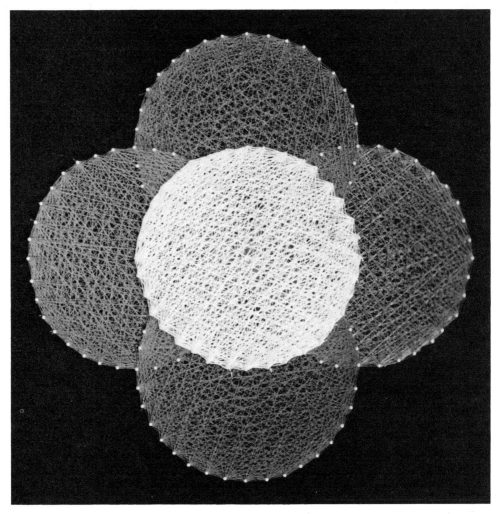

Figure 78   Circle Flower design.

circles. You can work the circles in any size; but each circle should have 36 equally spaced brads.

If you are using a real fine thread, you may want to thread more layers than shown here. The completed design in Figure 78 was worked with red and yellow wool knitting thread on a bright orange felt background board, 16″ × 24″.

Making Your Design Pattern

Using Figure 79 as a guide, draw five circles of the same diameter, overlapping them as shown in the pattern. The best, most accurate way of drawing circles is with a compass. If you do not have a compass the following technique works very well.

Using string and a pencil, tie the string in a slip knot around the pencil and pull tight. Lay the pattern to be marked on a flat surface

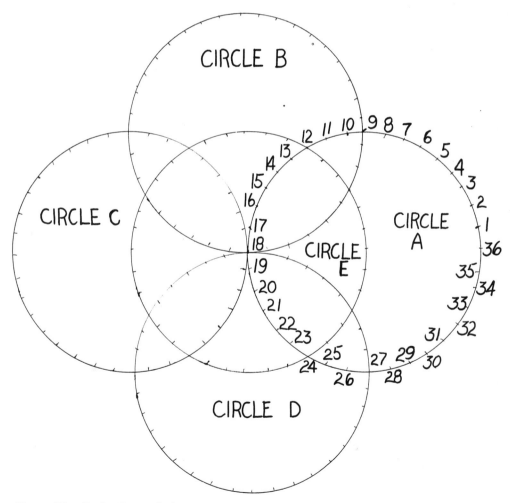

Figure 79   Circle Flower design pattern.

and have a ruler handy. Holding the pencil vertically and at the zero end of the ruler, measure the length of string to equal the radius (half of the diameter) of the circle you wish to draw. Pinch the loose end of the string at the required length and hold it at the point which will be the center of the circle. Hold the pencil and string firmly and swing the pencil point in an arc, thus marking your circle.

Your overall design should be approximately 13½″ high and 13½″ wide. Label your circles A, B, C, D, and E. Place and label 36 equally spaced brads on each circle (see Fig. 79).

Working the Threading Pattern

Since each circle has 36 brads, each circle will have 18 threading sequences. All five circles will be threaded alike and in the following order: circle A, circle B, circle C, circle D, and circle E.

The threading pattern is worked as follows:

1. Tie your thread at brad 1; then pull to 2-36-3-35-4-34-5-33-6-32-7-31-8-30-9-29-10-28-11-27-12-26-13-25-14-24-15-23-16-22-17-21-18-20-19. Tie off.

2. Tie your thread at brad 2; then pull to 1-3-36-4-35-5-34-6-33-7-32-8-31-9-30-10-29-11-28-12-27-13-26-14-25-15-24-16-23-17-22-18-21-19-20. Tie off.

3. Tie your thread at brad 3; then pull to 2-4-1-5-36-6-35-7-34-8-33-9-32-10-31-11-30-12-29-13-28-14-27-15-26-16-25-17-24-18-23-19-22-20-21. Tie off.

4. Tie your thread at brad 4; then pull to 3-5-2-6-1-7-36-8-35-9-34-10-33-11-32-12-31-13-30-14-29-15-28-16-27-17-26-18-25-19-24-20-23-21-22. Tie off.

5. Tie your thread at brad 5; then pull to 4-6-3-7-2-8-1-9-36-10-35-11-34-12-33-13-32-14-31-15-30-16-29-17-28-18-27-19-26-20-25-21-24-22-23. Tie off.

6. Tie your thread at brad 6; then pull to 5-7-4-8-3-9-2-10-1-11-36-12-35-13-34-14-33-15-32-16-31-17-30-18-29-19-28-20-27-21-26-22-25-23-24. Tie off.

7. Tie your thread at brad 7; then pull to 6-8-5-9-4-10-3-11-2-12-1-13-36-14-35-15-34-16-33-17-32-18-31-19-30-20-29-21-28-22-27-23-26-24-25. Tie off.

8. Tie your thread at brad 8; then pull to 7-9-6-10-5-11-4-12-3-13-2-14-1-15-36-16-35-17-34-18-33-19-32-20-31-21-30-22-29-23-28-24-27-25-26. Tie off.

9. Tie your thread at brad 9; then pull to 8-10-7-11-6-12-5-13-4-14-3-15-2-16-1-17-36-18-35-19-34-20-33-21-32-22-31-23-30-24-29-25-28-26-27. Tie off.

10. Tie your thread at brad 10; then pull to 9-11-8-12-7-13-6-14-5-15-4-16-3-17-2-18-1-19-36-20-35-21-34-22-33-23-32-24-31-25-30-26-29-27-28. Tie off.

11. Tie your thread at brad 11; then pull to 10-12-9-13-8-14-7-15-6-16-5-17-4-18-3-19-2-20-1-21-36-22-35-23-34-24-33-25-32-26-31-27-30-28-29. Tie off.

12. Tie your thread at brad 12; then pull to 11-13-10-14-9-15-8-16-7-17-6-18-5-19-4-20-3-21-2-22-1-23-36-24-35-25-34-26-33-27-32-28-31-29-30. Tie off.

13. Tie your thread at brad 13; then pull to 12-14-11-15-10-16-9-17-8-18-7-19-6-20-5-21-4-22-3-23-2-24-1-25-36-26-35-27-34-28-33-29-32-30-31. Tie off.

14. Tie your thread at brad 14; then pull to 13-15-12-16-11-17-10-18-9-19-8-20-7-21-6-22-5-23-4-24-3-25-2-26-1-27-36-28-35-29-34-30-33-31-32. Tie off.

15. Tie your thread at brad 15; then pull to 14-16-13-17-12-18-11-19-10-20-9-21-8-22-7-23-6-24-5-25-4-26-3-27-2-28-1-29-36-30-35-31-34-32-33. Tie off.

16. Tie your thread at brad 16; then pull to 15-17-14-18-13-19-12-20-11-21-10-22-9-23-8-24-7-25-6-26-5-27-4-28-3-29-2-30-1-31-36-32-35-33-34. Tie off.

17. Tie your thread at brad 17; then pull to 16-18-15-19-14-20-13-21-12-22-11-23-10-24-9-25-8-26-7-27-6-28-5-29-4-30-3-31-2-32-1-33-36-34-35. Tie off.

18. Tie your thread at brad 18; then pull to 17-19-16-20-15-21-14-22-13-23-12-24-11-25-10-26-9-27-8-28-7-29-6-30-5-31-4-32-3-33-2-34-1-35-36. Tie off.

Repeat this threading pattern, steps 1 to 18, for each circle.

Flamingo

The Flamingo is a tall structural bird with very long legs and a long neck. The flamingo bird as viewed in nature is found around water, wading and stirring up the bottom with restless feet searching for food. This is an excellent design for a child's room.

To capture the bird in string, every effort is made to provide a natural setting (see color section). This design should be worked on a black or rich blue background with the flamingo in a vivid pink thread and the water in a contrasting blue. Velvet for the background and crochet yarn for stringing is suggested.

Exposed brads are used for the long and elegant S-shaped neck, the bill, the tail, and the leg sections. The overall dimensions of the board used for this project as shown in the color section are 16" × 24"; the overall size of the design itself is 8" × 13". All brads should be placed about ¼" apart.

Making Your Design Pattern

To enlarge this pattern, trace the design in Figure 80 onto ½" graph paper. Now, working square by square, transfer the Flamingo design from the ½" graph paper to 1" graph paper. Using the dimensions given in Figure 81 for the water, draw the water lines on your pattern and label them A, B, C, D and E (Use the project shown in the color section as a guide for proper placement of water lines).

Number the brad points in the circle for the body 1 to 24; number the brad points in the circle for the head 1 to 18 as shown. The brads on the body should be about ½" apart; the brads on the head should be about ¼" apart.

Your pattern should now be about 13" high and 8" wide. It is now ready to be used.

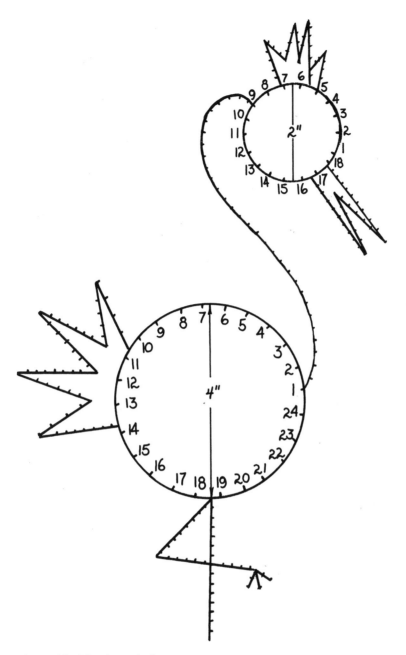

Figure 80 Flamingo design.

Working the Threading Pattern

The threading for the head and body circles are worked the same as the Circle Flower threading sequence (see Figs. 78 and 79). The Flamingo body has 24 brads, so you work the threading 12 times, starting at brads 1 to 12; the Flamingo head section has 18 brads, so you work the threading 9 times, starting at brads 1 to 9.

101

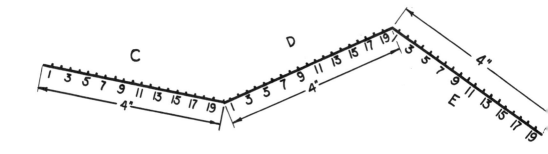

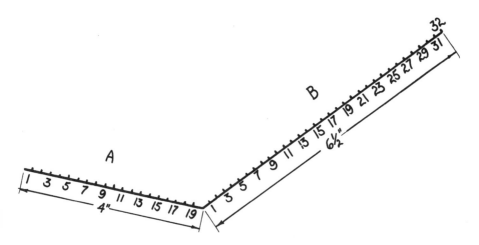

Figure 81   Design pattern for water lines for Flamingo design.

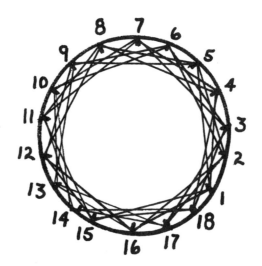

Figure 82   Optional threading pattern for Flamingo head.

102

Work the *Flamingo body* following this pattern.

1. Tie your thread at brad 1 and follow this sequence: 1-2; 2-24; 24-3; 3-23; 23-4; 4-22; 22-5; 5-21; 21-6; 6-20; 20-7; 7-19; 19-8; 8-18; 18-9; 9-17; 17-10; 10-16; 16-11; 11-15; 15-12; 12-14; 14-13. Tie off.

2. Tie at brad 2 and continue to 3-1-4-24-5-23-6-22-7-21-8-20-9-19-10-18-11-17-12-16-13-15-14. Tie off.

3. Tie at brad 3 and continue to 4-2-5-1-6-24-7-23-8-22-9-21-10-20-11-19-12-18-12-17-14-16-15. Tie off.

4. Tie at brad 4 then to 5-3-6-2-7-1-8-24-9-23-10-22-11-21-12-20-13-19-14-18-15-17-16. Tie off.

5. Tie at brad 5, then to 6-4-7-3-8-2-9-1-10-24-11-23-12-22-13-21-14-20-15-19-16-18-17. Tie off.

6. Tie at brad 6, then to 7-5-8-4-9-3-10-2-11-1-12-24-13-23-14-22-15-21-16-20-17-19-18. Tie off.

7. Tie at brad 7, then to 8-6-9-5-10-4-11-3-12-2-13-1-14-24-15-23-16-22-17-21-18-20-19. Tie off.

8. Tie at brad 8, then to 9-7-10-6-11-5-12-4-13-3-14-2-15-1-16-24-17-23-18-22-19-21-20. Tie off.

9. Tie at brad 9, then to 10-8-11-7-12-6-13-5-14-4-15-3-16-2-17-1-18-24-19-23-20-22-21. Tie off.

10. Tie at brad 10, then to 11-9-12-8-13-7-14-6-15-5-16-4-17-3-18-2-19-1-20-24-21-23-22. Tie off.

11. Tie at brad 11, then to 12-10-13-9-14-8-15-7-16-6-17-5-18-4-19-1-20-2-21-1-22-24-23. Tie off.

12. Tie at brad 12, then to 13-11-14-10-15-9-16-8-17-7-18-6-19-5-20-4-21-3-22-2-23-1-24. Tie off.

Work the *Flamingo head section,* following this threading pattern:

Tie your thread at brad 1; 1-2; 2-18; 18-3; 3-17; 17-4; 4-16; 16-5; 5-15; 15-6; 6-14; 14-7; 7-13; 13-8; 8-12; 12-9; 9-11; 11-1. Tie off. Continue stringing in this pattern, rotating each starting brad from 2 to 9, consecutively. Remember there are only 18 brads in the head section, therefore you will have 9 ties. In the body section, there were 24 brads and the threading pattern called for 12 ties.

For an *optional* threading which will give more depth to the *head section* (Fig. 82), tie your thread at brad 1 and follow this sequence: 1-4; 4-2; 2-5; 5-3; 3-6; 6-4; 4-7; 7-5; 5-8; 8-6; 6-9; 9-7; 7-10; 10-8; 8-11; 11-9; 9-12; 12-10; 10-13; 13-11; 11-14; 14-12; 12-15; 15-13; 13-16; 16-14; 14-17; 17-15; 15-18; 18-16; 16-1; 1-17; 17-2; 2-18; 18-3. Tie off.

Work the *water lines A and B* (Fig. 81) with the one-to-one correspondence method. However, in order to complete the threading on the longer line B, a doubling technique must be used. First thread brads 1 to 19, using the one-to-one correspondence method (1-1; 1-2; 2-2; 2-3 . . . 18-18; 18-19; 19-19); *do not tie off.* Now, work the doubling effect pattern: from brad 19 on line B, string the thread to brad 18 on line A; 18-20; 20-17; 17-21; 21-16; 16-22; 22-15; 15-23; 23-14; 14-24; 24-13; 13-25; 25-12; 12-26; 26-11; 11-27; 27-10; 10-28; 28-9; 9-29; 29-8; 8-30; 30-7; 7-31; 31-6; 6-32. Tie off. Note the diamond-like pattern formed on the doubling thread section.

Work *water lines C, D, and E* with the one-to-one overthreading and underthreading pattern (see Fig. 15).

Sharpie the Cruiser

Sharpie the Cruiser, as shown in the color section, was worked on a light blue felt background fabric with white crochet thread for the sails and black polyester thread for the boat. The overall dimension of the board it was worked on is 24″ × 24″.

Making Your Design Pattern

To enlarge the pattern for this design, trace Figures 83 and 84 onto ½″ graph paper. Now, working line by line and square by square, transfer the design onto 1″ graph paper. Your pattern should now be full size, approximately 17½″ at the highest point and 15″ at the widest point.

Label and place all brads about ¼″ apart. To join your two pattern pieces (Figs. 83 and 84), line up the top of the mast pole in Figure 84 with the point marked X on the bottom of sail 2 in Figure 83. These eight brads are left free of thread to form the mast pole.

Working the Threading Pattern

All three sails are threaded with the one-to-one correspondence method; each sail will have a twisting pattern to give the effect of billowing sails.

1.   To work the *first layer on sail 1*, follow this sequence (see Fig. 85). Tie your thread at brad X; pull thread tight to XX; work the top and bottom of the sail; XX-12; 12-1; 1-11; 11-2; 2-10; 10-3; 3-9; 9-4; 4-8; 8-5; 5-7; 7-6; 6-6; 6-7; 7-5; 5-8; 8-4; 4-9; 9-3; 3-10; 10-2; 2-11; 11-1; 1-12; 12-Z; Z-13; 13-1 on the left side; 1-14 on the bottom; 14-2; 2-15; 15-3; 3-16; 16-4; 4-17. Tie off.

2.   To work the *second layer on sail 1,* follow this sequence (see Fig. 85). Tie your thread at brad 9(Y); pull to brad 5(YY); 5(YY)-10 on the right side: 10-4; 4-11; 11-3; 3-12; 12-2; 2-13; 13-1; 1-14; 14-Z; Z-15;

105

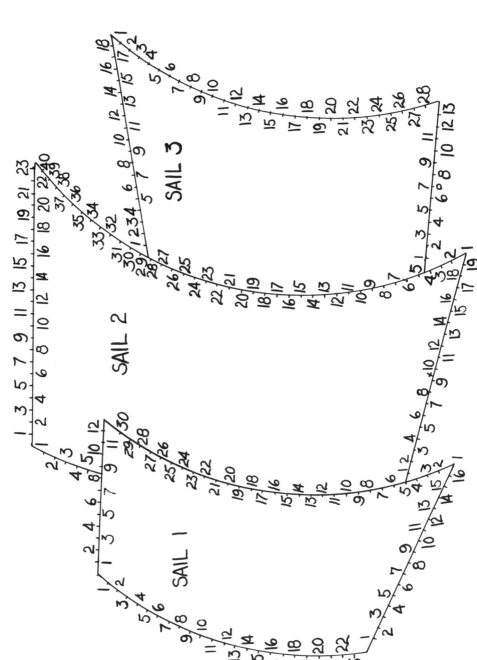

Figure 83 Sharpie the Cruiser pattern for sails.

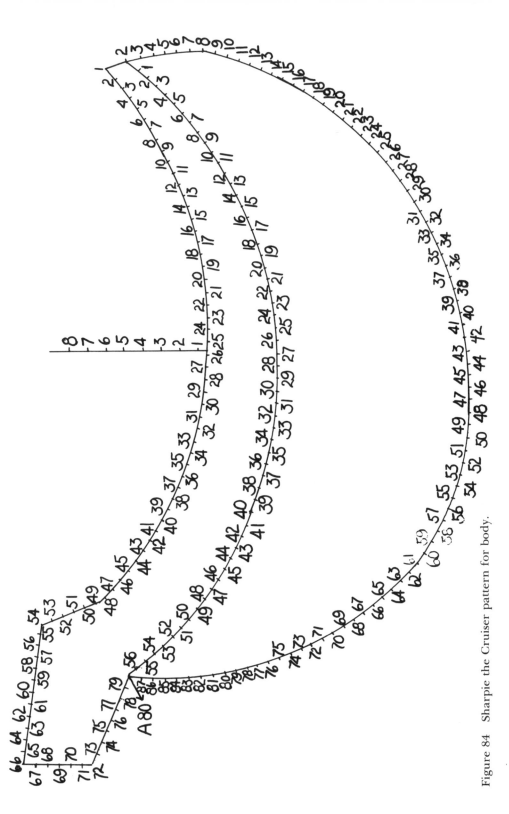

Figure 84 Sharpie the Cruiser pattern for body.

107

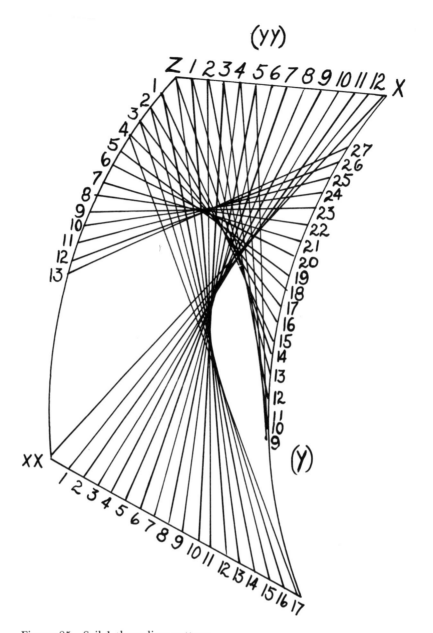

Figure 85   Sail 1 threading pattern.

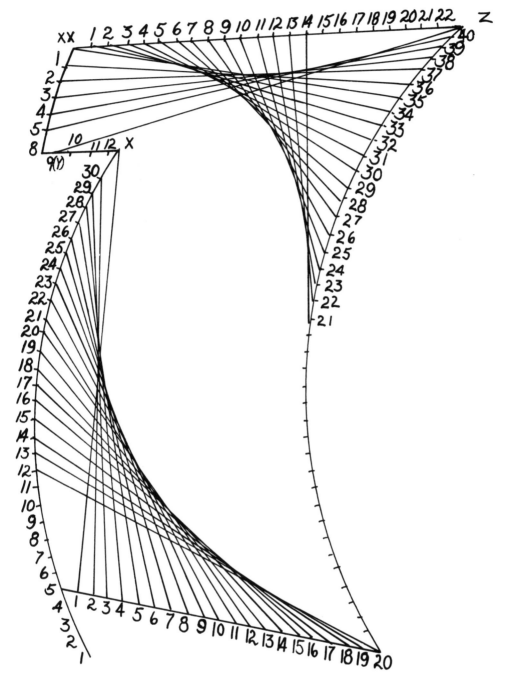

Figure 86   Sail 2 threading pattern.

15-1 on the left side; 1-16; 16-2; 2-17; 17-3; 3-18; 18-4; 4-19; 19-5; 5-20; 20-6; 6-21; 21-7; 7-22; 22-8; 8-23; 23-9; 9-24; 24-10; 10-25; 25-11; 11-26; 26-12; 12-17; 27-13. Tie off here (as shown in Fig. 85); or if you wish, continue this threading pattern in a counterclockwise direction to cover the sail completely (as shown in the color section).

3.   To work the *bottom of sail 2,* follow this sequence (see Fig. 86). Tie your thread at brad 12(X); pull to brad 1 on the bottom line; work the left and bottom sides of the sail: 1-30; 30-2; 2-29; 29-3; 3-28; 28-4; 4-27; 27-5; 5-26; 26-6; 6-25; 25-7; 7-24; 24-8; 8-23; 23-9; 9-22; 22-10; 10-21; 21-11; 11-20; 20-12; 12-19; 19-13; 13-18; 18-14; 14-17; 17-15; 15-16; 16-16; 16-15; 15-17; 17-14; 14-18; 18-13; 13-19; 19-12; 12-20. Tie off here (as shown in Fig. 86); or continue to thread in this twisting thread pattern to completely cover the bottom of sail 2 (as shown in the color section).

4.   To work the *top of sail 2,* follow this sequence (see Fig. 86). Tie your thread at brad 9(Y); pull to brad Z; work up the left side from Y and down the right: Z-8; 8-40; 40-5; 5-39; 39-4; 4-38; 38-3; 3-37; 37-2; 2-36; 36-1; 1-35; 35-XX; XX-34; 34-1; on the top side; 1-33 on the right; 33-2; 2-32; 32-3; 3-31; 31-4; 4-30; 30-5; 5-29; 29-6; 6-28; 28-7; 7-27; 27-8; 8-26; 26-9; 9-25; 25-10; 10-24; 24-11; 11-23; 23-12; 12-22; 22-13; 13-21; 21-14. Tie off.

5.   To work the *first layer of sail 3,* follow this sequence (see Fig. 87). Tie your thread at brad 28 at the upper left corner; pull to brad 29 at the lower right corner; work the right and left sides: 29-27; 27-28; 28-26; 26-27; 27-25; 25-26; 26-24; 24-25; 25-23; 23-24; 24-22; 22-23; 23-21; 21-22; 22-20; 20-21; 21-19; 19-20; 20-18; 18-19; 19-17; 17-18; 18-16; 16-17; 17-15; 15-16; 16-14; 14-15; 15-13; 13-14; 14-12; 12-13; 13-11; 11-12; 12-10; 10-11; 11-9; 9-10; 10-8; 8-9; 9-7; 7-8; 8-6; 6-7; 7-5; 5-6; 6-4; 4-5. Tie off.

6.   To work the *second layer of sail 3,* follow this sequence (see Fig. 87). Tie your thread at brad 19 in the upper right corner; work the top and left sides: 19-27; 27-18; 18-26; 26-17; 17-25; 25-16; 16-24; 24-15; 15-23; 23-14; 14-22; 22-13; 13-21; 21-12; 12-20; 20-11; 11-19; 19-10; 10-18; 18-9; 9-17; 17-8; 8-16; 16-7; 7-15; 15-6; 6-14; 14-5; 5-13; 13-4; 4-12; 12-3; 3-11; 11-2; 2-10; 10-1. Tie off.

7.   To work the *third layer on sail 3,* follow this sequence (see Fig. 87). Tie your thread at brad 28 on the upper left corner; pull to brad 1 on the bottom line; work the left side with the bottom and right sides: 1-27 on the left; 27-2; 2-26; 26-3; 3-25; 25-4; 4-24; 24-5; 5-23; 23-6; 6-22; 22-7; 7-21; 21-8; 8-20; 20-9; 9-19; 19-10; 10-18; 18-11;

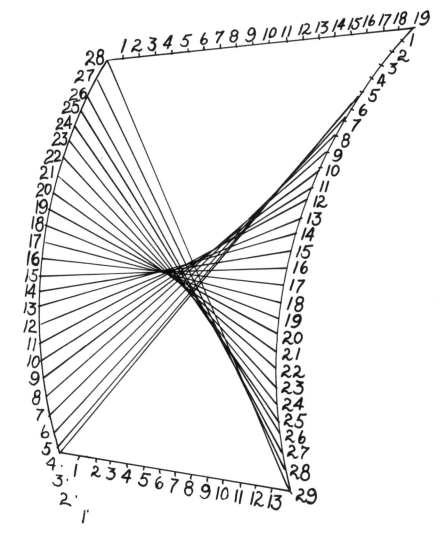

Figure 87   Sail 3 threading pattern.

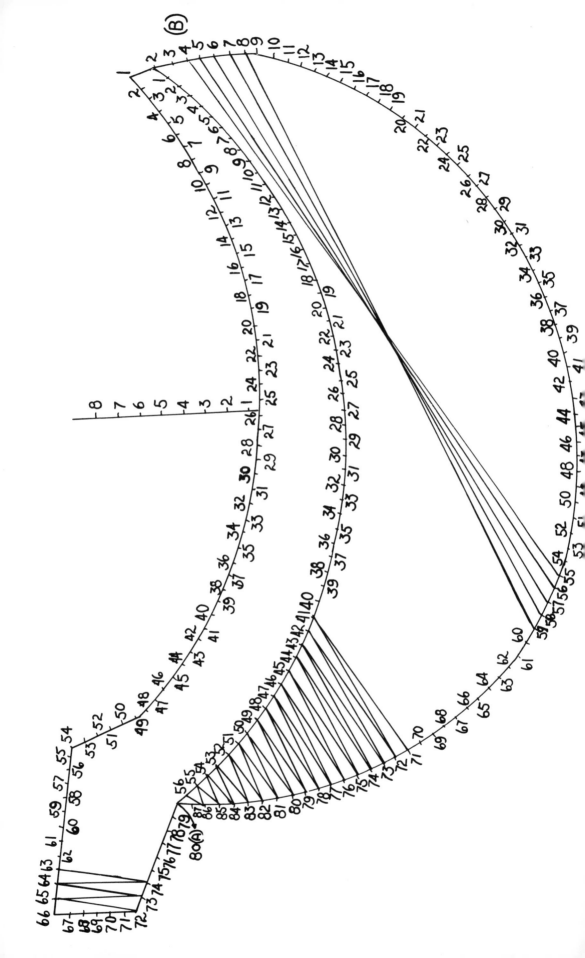

(B)

11-17; 17-12; 12-16; 16-13; 13-15; 15-29 at the bottom right corner; 29-14 on the left; 14-28 on the right; 28-13; 13-27; 27-12; 12-26; 26-11; 11-25; 25-10; 10-24; 24-9; 9-23; 23-8; 8-22; 22-7; 7-21; 21-6; 6-20; 20-5; 5-19; 19-4. Tie off.

8.   If you wish, repeat any of these threading sequences to add depth to the overall effect.

9.   To work the *top section of the body,* follow this sequence (see Fig. 88). Tie your thread at brad 72 in the bottom left corner of the top body section; pull to brad 65 on the top line; work the diagonal threading pattern (see Fig. 14): 65-73; 73-64; 64-74; 74-63; 63-75; 75-62; 62-76; 76-61; 61-77; 77-60; 60-78; 78-59; 59-79; 79-58; 58-80(A); 80(A)-57; 57-56; 56-56; 56-55; 55-55; 55-54; 54-54; 54-53; 53-53; 53-52; 52-52 . . . work this one-to-one method to the end, 1-1. Tie off.

10.   To work the *base or bottom section of the body,* follow this sequence (see Fig. 88). Tie your thread at brad 56 at the top left corner of the base; pull to brad 86 on the bottom line of the body; work the diagonal threading across the base: 86-55; 55-85; 85-54; 54-84; 84-53; 53-83; 83-52; 52-82; 82-51; 51-81; 81-50; 50-80 . . . continue working in this sequence to the upper right corner of the base.

11.   To work the *second layer on the base,* follow this sequence (see Fig. 88). Tie your thread at brad 4(B) on the upper right corner; pull to brad 55 on the bottom line of the body; 55-5; 5-56; 56-6; 6-57; 57-7; 7-58 . . . continue this sequence to the other side of the base at brad 80(A). Tie off.

Panda

This lovable Panda design pictured in the color section is threaded in three sections: head and neck; body, arm, and shoulder; and lower leg. The board it was worked on is 24″ × 24″. The background is light brown felt and threading was worked with dark brown cotton cord.

Making Your Design Pattern

Using Figure 89, trace the Panda design onto ¼″ graph paper. Now, working line by line and square by square, transfer the design to 1″ graph paper. Your pattern should now be full size, approximately 19½″ at the highest point and 16½″ at the widest point.

Using Figures 89 to 93 as a guide, place and carefully label all brads.

Working Your Threading Pattern

Work the *neck and head section* (Fig. 90), following this sequence.

1. Tie your thread at brad 75 on the left ear; pull tight to brad 110 on the lower side of the face; pull to brad A on the side of the face; loop around and return to 109; 109-B; B-108; 108-C; C-107; 107-D; D-106; 106-E; E-105; 105-F; F-104; 104-110; 110-75; 75-74; 74-A; A-73; 73-B; B-72; 72-C; C-71; 71-D; D-70; E-69; 69-F; F-75; 75-200; 200-74; 74-201; 201-73; 73-202; 202-72; 202-203; 203-71; 71-204; 204-70; 70-205; 205-69; 67-206; 206-68; 68-207; 207-68; 68-205; 205-67. Tie off.

2. Tie your thread at brad 123; pull tight to brad G; loop and return to brad 122; 122-H; H-121; 121-I; I-120; 120-J; J-119; 119-K; K-118; 118-L; L-117; 117-M; M-116; 116-N; N-115; 115-O; O-114; O-128. Tie off.

3. Tie your thread at brad 138; pull tight to brad G; loop and return to brad 137; 137-F; F-136; 136-E; E-135; 135-D; D-134;

114

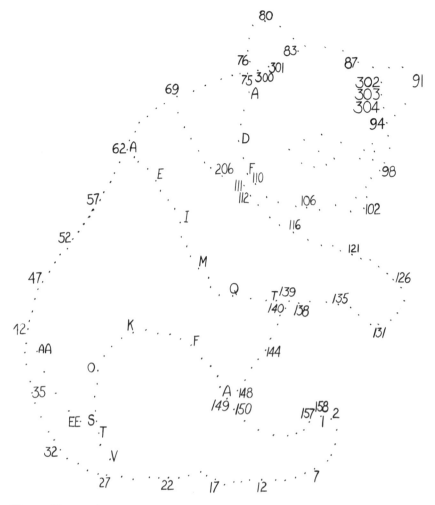

Figure 89 Panda design pattern.

134-C; C-133; 133-B; B-132; 132-A; A-131; 131-63; 63-130; 130-64; 64-129; 129-65. Tie off.

4. Tie your thread at brad O; pull thread tight to brad 128; loop and return to brad P; P-127; 127-Q; Q-126; 126-R; R-125; 125-S; S-124; 124-T; T-123; 123-139; 139-122; 122-138; 138-121; 121-137; 137-120; 120-136; 136-119; 119-135; 135-118; 118-134; 134-117; 117-133; 133-116; 116-132; 132-66; 66-131. Tie off.

5. For the *left ear section,* you may glue in a piece of felt rather than thread this section. If you prefer to continue threading the brads, work the lattice method (see Fig. 13b) as follows: Tie your thread at 79; 79-80; 80-78; 78-81; 81-77; 77-82; 82-76; 76-83. Tie off.

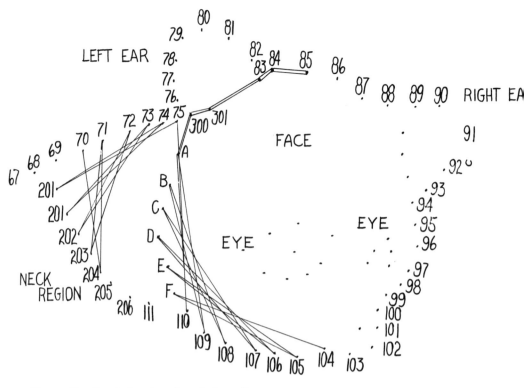

Figure 90   Panda head and neck threading pattern.

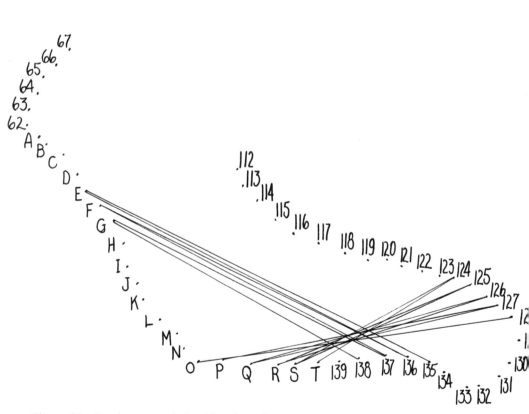

Figure 91   Panda arm and shoulder threading pattern.

116

6. For the *right ear section,* work this threading pattern: 90-91; 91-89; 89-92; 92-88; 88-93; 93-94; 94-89. Tie off.

7. The *face section* is left free of thread on the inside and is outlined with a chain loop pattern on the border: Tie your thread at brad A; pull to brad 300; loop and return to brad A; pull to brad 301; loop and return to brad 300; loop and pull to brad 83; loop and

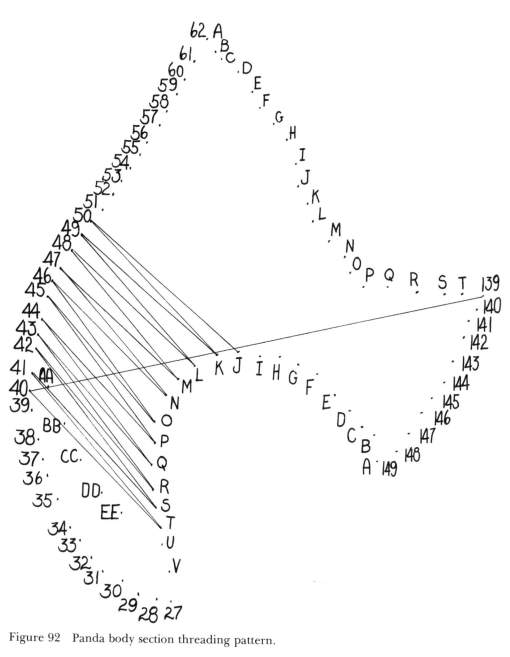

Figure 92   Panda body section threading pattern.

return to brad 301; loop and pull to brad 84; loop and return to brad 83; loop and pull to brad 85; loop and return to brad 84; 84-86; 86-85; 85-87; 87-86; 86-88; 88-87; 87-302; 302-88; 88-303; 303-302; 302-304; 304-303; 303-94; 94-304; 304-95; 95-94; 94-96; 96-95; 95-97; 97-96; 96-98; 98-97; 97-99; 99-98; 98-100; 100-99; 99-101; 101-100; 100-102; 102-104; 104-103; 103-110; loop and return to brad A. Tie off.

8. The eyes are outlined in brads with a large brass tack as the pupil. Also a brass tack is used for the nose. No threading is necessary here.

Now, work the *body, arm, and shoulder section* (Figs. 91 and 92), following this sequence.

1. Tie your thread at brad 139; pull tight to brad 40; loop around and return to brad T on the upper leg; loop around and pull to brad 41; loop around and pull to brad S on the upper leg; S-42; 42-R; R-43; 43-Q; Q-44; 44-P; P-45; 45-O; O-46; 46-N; N-47; 47-M; M-48; 48-L; L-49; 49-K; K-50; 50-J; J-51; 51-I; I-52; 52-H; H-53; 53-G; G-54; 54-F; F-55; 55-E; E-56; 56-D; D-57; 57-C; C-58; 58-B; B-59; 59-62(A); loop brad 62 (A) twice and pull to brad 40; 40-B; B-39; 39-C; C-AA; AA-D; D-38; 38-E; E-BB; BB-F; F-AA; AA-G; N-H; H-M; M-I; I-L; L-J; J-K; K-K; K-J; J-L; L-I; I-M; M-H; H-N; N-G;

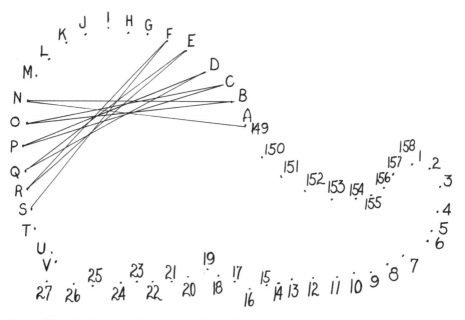

Figure 93 Panda lower leg section threading pattern.

G-O; O-F; F-P; P-E; E-Q; Q-D; D-R; R-C; C-S; S-B; B-T; T-B; B-139; 139-C; C-140; 140-D; D-141; 141-E; E-142; 142-F; F-143; 143-G; G-144; 144-H; H-145; 145-E; E-146; 146-R; on the upper leg; R-147; 147-Q; Q-148; 148-P; P-149; 149-O. Tie off.

2. Work the *tail section* in a diagonal or horizontal lattice thread-ing pattern: Tie your thread at brad 40; pull tight to brad AA; AA-39; 39-BB; BB-38; 38-CC; CC-37; 37-36; 36-DD; DD-35; 35-EE. Tie off, or work this same pattern until the tail threading is as heavy as you like.

Now, work the *lower leg section* (Fig. 93), following this sequence.

1. Tie your thread at brad 149(A); pull thread tight to brad N; loop around and pull to brad B; B-O; O-C; C-P; P-D; D-Q; Q-E; E-R; R-F; F-S; S-G; G-T; T-H; H-U; U-I; I-V; V-J; J-26; 26-K; K-25; 25-L; L-24; 24-M; M-23; 23-N; N-22; 22-O; O-21; 21-P; P-20; 20-Q; Q-19; 19-R; R-18; 18-1; 1-17; 17-2; 2-16; 16-3; 3-15; 15-4; 4-14; 14-5; 5-13; 13-6. Tie off.

2. Tie your thread at brad 149 and follow this sequence for a double lattice pattern for the entire leg: 149-T; T-150; 150-U; U-151; 151-V; V-152; 152-26; 26-153; 153-25; 25-154; 154-24; 24-155; 155-23; 23-156; 156-22; 22-157; 157-21; 21-157. Tie off.

3. Tie your thread at brad 6; pull tight to brad 157; 157-7; 7-156; 156-8; 8-155; 155-9; 9-154; 154-10; 10-153; 153-11; 11-152; 152-12; 12-151; 151-13; 13-150; 150-14; 14-149; 149-15; 15-B; B-16; 16-C; C-17; 17-D; D-18; 18-E; E-19; 19-F; F-20; 20-G; G-21; 21-H; H-22; 22-I; I-23; 23-J; J-24; 24-K; K-25; 25-L; L-26; 26-M; M-V. Tie off.

Quadrilateral Composition

This interesting design of straight lines worked with overlapping thread patterns makes a striking wall hanging. The finished project shown in the color section was worked in gold polyester thread on a red velvet background board, 24″ × 24″.

This design can be worked in a monochromatic scheme or in two highly contrasting colors.

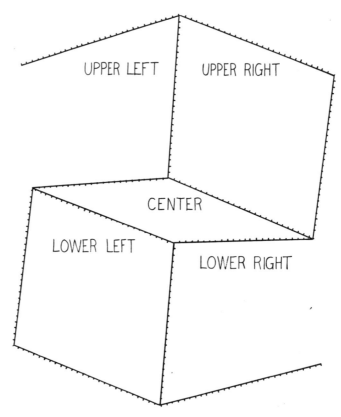

Figure 94   Quadrilateral Composition design pattern.

Making Your Design Pattern

To enlarge the pattern in Figure 94, trace the design onto ¼"
graph paper. Working line by line and square by square, transfer the
design to 1" graph paper.

Your pattern should now be full size, approximately 13½" at the
widest point and 14½" at the highest point.

Using Figures 95 to 98 as a guide, label and place all brads about ¼"
apart.

Working the Threading Pattern

The threading for this project is worked in the one-to-one correspondence method.

1.   To work the *top right section* (see Fig. 95) design, follow this
sequence. Tie your thread at brad 1 on A; 1-1; 1-2; 2-2; 2-3; 3-3; 3-4;
4-4; 4-5; 5-5; 5-6; 6-6; 6-7; 7-7; 7-8; 8-8; 8-9; 9-9; 9-10; 10-10; 10-11;
11-11; 11-12; 12-12; 12-13; 13-13; 13-14; 14-14; 14-15; 15-15; 15-16;
16-16; 16-17; 17-17; 17-18; 18-18; 19-19; 19-20; 20-20; 20-21; 21-21;
21-22; 22-22; 22-23; 23-23; 23-24; 24-24; 24-25; 25-25; 25-26; 26-26;
27-27; 27-28. Tie off.

Now, thread line C with line D, following the above one-to-one
correspondence method.

These threading sequences must be worked two times—once for
the top right section and one for the *lower left section.*

2.   To work the *upper left section* (see Fig. 96), follow this sequence.
Thread line A with line B: Tie your thread at brad 1 on A; 1-1; 1-2;
2-2; 2-3; 3-3; 3-4; 4-4; 4-5; 5-5; 5-6; 6-6; 6-7; 7-7; 7-8; 8-8; 8-9; 9-9;
9-10; 10-10; 10-11; 11-11; 11-12; 12-12; 12-13; 13-13; 13-14; 14-14;
14-15; 15-15; 15-16; 16-16; 16-17; 17-17; 17-18; 18-18; 18-19; 19-19;
19-20; 20-20; 20-21; 21-21; 21-22; 22-22; 22-23; 23-23; 23-24; 24-24;
24-25; 25-25; 25-26; 26-26; 26-27; 27-27; 27-28. Tie off.

Now, thread line B with line C, following the above sequence. Start
this threading at brad 1 on B and pull to brad 1 on C; 1-2;
2-2 . . . work this till 23-23; 23-24 on line B. Tie off.

3.   To work the *lower right section* (see Fig. 97), follow this sequence. Thread line A with line B: Tie your thread at brad 1 on line
A; 1-1; 1-2; 2-2; 2-3; 3-3; 3-4; 4-4; 4-5; 5-5; 5-6; 6-6; 6-7; 7-7; 7-8;
8-8; 8-9; 9-9; 9-10; 10-10; 10-11; 11-11; 11-12; 12-12; 12-13; 13-13;
13-14; 14-14; 14-15; 15-15; 15-16; 16-16; 16-17; 17-17; 17-18; 18-18;
18-19; 19-19; 19-20; 20-20; 20-21; 21-21; 21-22; 22-22; 22-23; 23-23;

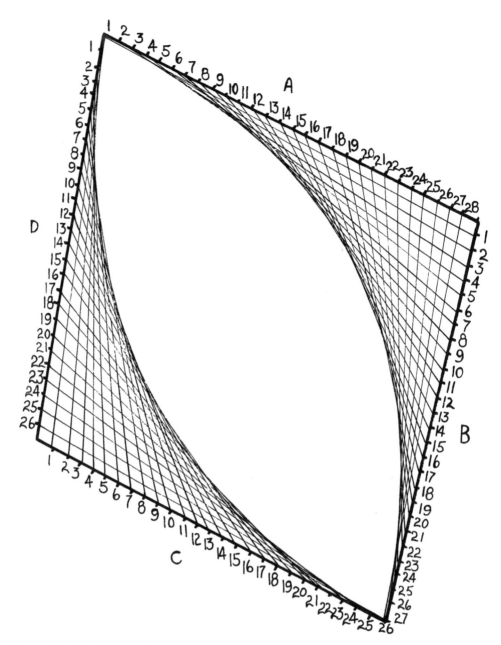

Figure 95   Quadrilateral Composition threading pattern for top right and lower left sections.

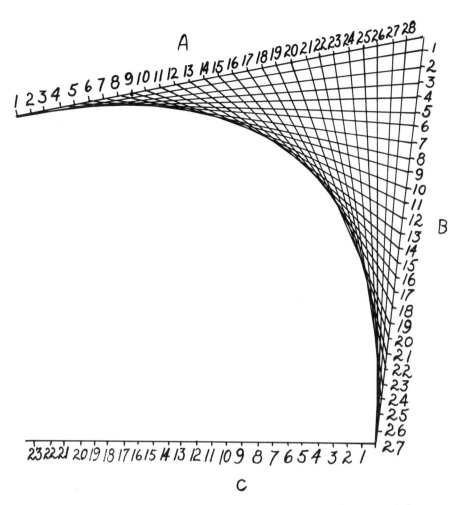

Figure 96   Quadrilateral Composition threading pattern for upper left section.

123

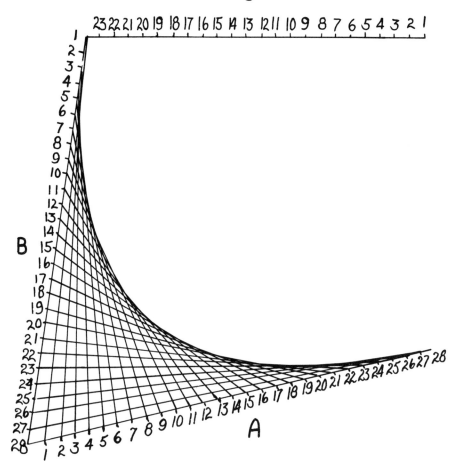

Figure 97 Quadrilateral Composition threading pattern for lower right section.

23-24; 24-24; 24-25; 25-25; 25-26; 26-26; 26-27; 27-27; 27-28. Tie off.

Now, thread line B with line C, following the above one-to-one correspondence method. Start this threading at brad 1 on line C and pull to brad 1 on line B; 1-2; 2-2 . . . work this till 23-23; 23-24. Tie off.

4. Now, work the *center section* (see Fig. 98) following this sequence. Tie your thread at brad 1 on line A; pull to brad 1 on line B; 1-2; 2-2; 2-3; 3-3; 3-4; 4-4; 4-5; 5-5; 5-6; 6-6; 6-7; 7-7; 7-8; 8-8; 8-9; 9-9; 9-10; 10-10; 10-11; 11-11; 11-12; 12-12; 12-13; 13-13; 13-14; 14-14; 14-15; 15-15; 15-16; 16-16; 16-17; 17-17; 17-18; 18-18; 18-19; 19-19; 19-20; 20-20; 20-21; 21-21; 21-22; 22-22; 22-23; 23-23. Tie off.

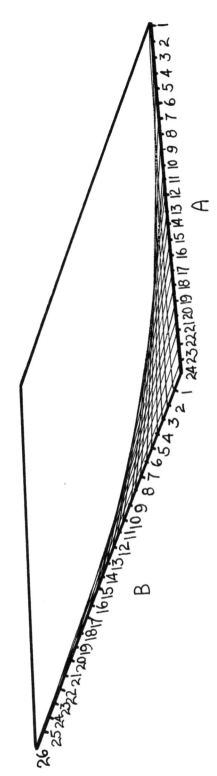

Figure 98 Quadrilateral Composition threading pattern for center section.

125

Peacock

The male peacock's enormous tail of brilliant colors and showy eyelike spots is one of nature's most spectacular displays.

The Peacock pictured in the color section was worked primarily in green with white and beige for the beak; the background, 24″ × 24″, is covered with black felt fabric.

Making Your Design Pattern

To enlarge the design in Figure 99, trace the design onto ¼″ graph paper. Now, working line by line and square by square, transfer the design to 1″ graph paper. Your pattern should now be full size, approximately 23″ at the highest point and 22″ at the widest.

Using Figure 100 for the "eyes" and Figure 104 for the head and breast section and Figure 106 for the beak section, mark and label for brad placement. On the long feathers which are left unthreaded, place your brads approximately ¼″ apart and ¼″ from the edge of the eye spots.

If you wish to work the design even larger than the one shown here, extend each feather and place the eyelike spots in position, according to personal taste and design elements. The eyes may be made larger or smaller without altering the overall appearance of the design. However, each eye should be threaded identically and the head and breast section according to the threading instructions given here.

Working the Threading Pattern

1. To work *layer 1 on the eye spots,* follow this sequence (see Fig. 100). Tie your thread at brad 1; pull tight to brad 13; loop around and work as follows: 13-2; 2-14; 14-31; 3-15; 15-4; 4-16; 16-5; 5-17; 17-6; 6-18; 18-7; 7-19; 19-8; 8-20; 20-9; 9-21; 21-10; 10-22; 22-11;

126

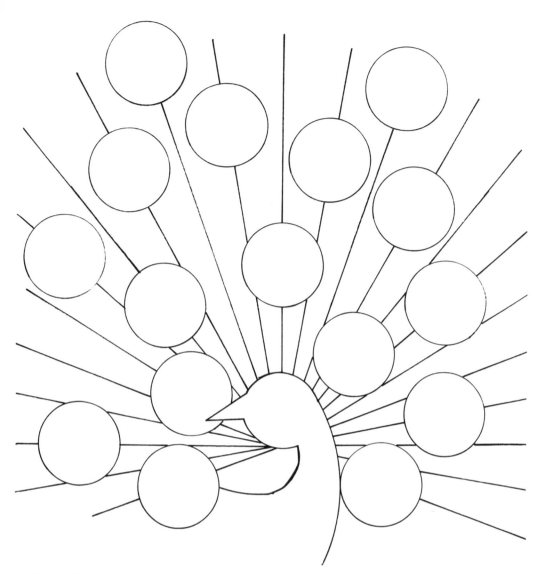

Figure 99   Peacock design.

11-23; 23-12; 12-24; 24-13; 13-25; 25-14; 14-26; 26-15; 15-27; 27-16; 16-28; 28-17; 17-29; 29-18; 18-30; 30-19; 19-31; 31-20; 20-32; 32-21; 21-33; 33-22; 22-34; 34-23; 23-35; 35-24; 24-36; 36-25; 25-1. Tie off.

2.   To work *layer 2 on the eye spots,* follow this sequence (see Fig. 101). Tie your thread at brad 1 and work as follows: 1-11; 11-2; 2-12; 12-3; 3-13; 13-4; 4-14; 14-5; 5-15; 15-6; 6-16; 16-7; 7-17; 17-8; 8-18; 18-9; 9-19; 19-10; 10-20; 20-11; 11-21; 21-12; 12-22; 22-13; 13-23; 23-14; 14-24; 24-15; 15-25; 25-16; 16-26; 26-17; 17-27; 27-18; 18-28;

127

28-19; 19-29; 29-20; 20-30; 30-21; 21-31; 31-22; 22-32; 32-23; 23-33; 33-24; 24-34; 34-25; 25-35; 35-26; 26-36; 36-27; 27-1. Tie off.

3.   To work *layer 3 on the eye spots,* follow this sequence (see Fig. 102). Tie your thread at brad 1 and work as follows: 1-9; 9-2; 2-10; 10-3; 3-11; 11-4; 4-12; 12-5; 5-13; 13-6; 6-14; 14-7; 7-15; 15-8; 8-16; 16-9; 9-17; 17-10; 10-18; 18-11; 11-19; 19-12; 12-20; 20-13; 13-21; 21-14; 14-22; 22-15; 15-23; 23-16; 16-24; 24-17; 17-25; 25-18; 18-26; 26-19; 19-27; 27-20; 20-28; 28-21; 21-29; 29-22; 22-30; 30-23; 23-31;

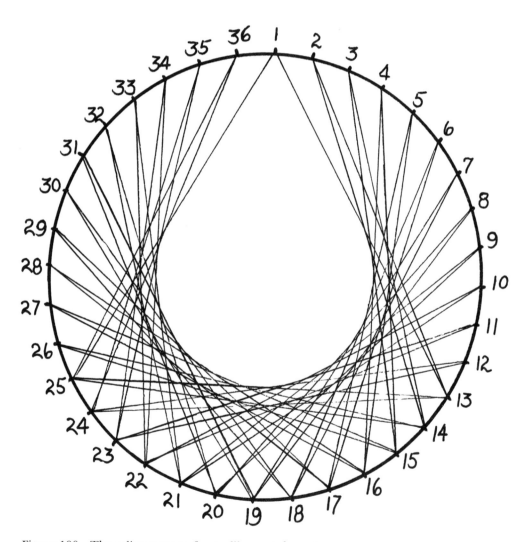

Figure 100   Threading pattern for eyelike spots layer 1.

31-24; 24-32; 32-25; 25-33; 33-26; 26-34; 34-27; 27-35; 35-28; 28-36; 36-29; 29-1. Tie off.

4.   To work *layer 4 on the eye spots,* follow this sequence. Tie your thread at brad 1 and work as follows: 1-7; 7-2; 2-8; 8-3; 3-9; 9-4; 4-10; 10-5; 5-11; 11-6; 6-12; 12-7; 7-13; 13-8; 8-14; 14-9; 9-15; 15-10; 10-16; 16-11; 11-17; 17-12; 12-18; 18-13; 13-19; 19-14; 14-20; 20-15; 15-21; 21-16; 16-22; 22-17; 17-23; 23-18; 18-24; 24-19; 19-25; 25-20; 20-26; 26-21; 21-27; 27-22; 22-28; 28-23; 23-29;29-24; 24-30; 30-25;

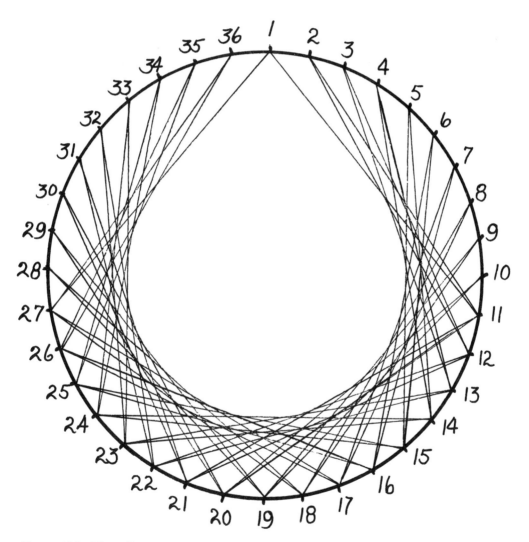

Figure 101   Threading pattern for eye spots, layer 2.

25-31; 31-26; 26-32; 32-27; 27-33; 33-28; 28-34; 34-29; 29-35; 35-30; 30-36; 36-31; 31-1. Tie off.

5.   To work the *head and breast section,* follow this sequence (see Fig. 104). Tie your thread at brad A1; pull tight to C1; C1-A2; A2-C2; C2-A3; A3-C3; C3-A4; A4-C4; C4-A5; A5-C5; C5-A6; A6-C6; C6-A7; A7-C7; C7-A8; A8-C8; C8-A9; A9-C9; C9-A10; A10-C10; C10-A11; A11-C11. Tie off.

Tie your thread again at D8; pull tight to Bl; Bl-D7; D7-B2; B2-D6;

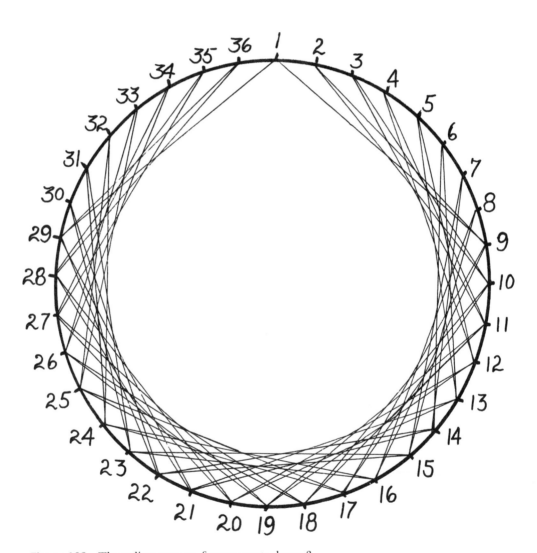

Figure 102   Threading pattern for eye spots, layer 3.

D6-B3; B3-D5; D5-B4; B4-D4; D4-B5; B5-D3; D3-B6; B6-D2; D2-B7; B7-D1; Dl-BB. Tie off.

Now work a diagonal threading pattern. Tie your thread at brad Al; pull tight to El; E1-A2; A2-E2; E2-A3; A3-E3; E3-A4; A4-E4; E4-A5; A5-E5; E5-A6; A6-E6; E6-A7; A7-E7; E7-A8; A8-E8; E8-A9; A9-E9; E9-A10; A10-E10; E10-A11; A11-E11; E11-A12; A12-E12; E12-A13; A13-E13; E13-A14; A14-E14; E14-A15; A15-E15; E15-B1; B1-E16; E16-B2; B2-E17; E17-B3; B3-E18; E18-B4;

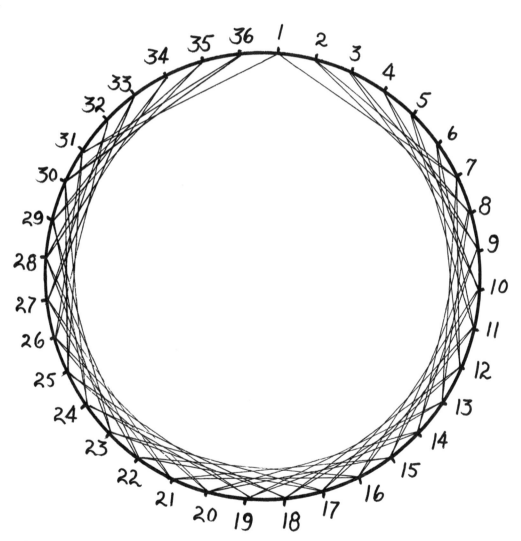

Figure 103   Threading pattern for eye spots, layer 4.

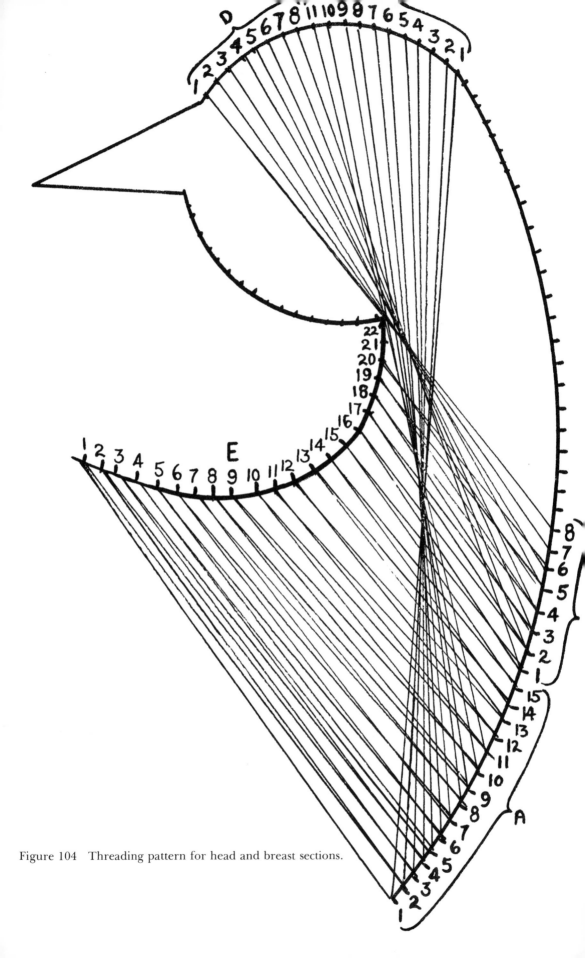

Figure 104   Threading pattern for head and breast sections.

B4-E19; E19-B5; B5-E20; E20-B6; B6-E21; E21-B7; B7-E22; E22-B8. Tie off.

Work the threading sequence for this section two times; use green thread for the first layer and blue for the second. If you wish to completely thread the neck section, continue your diagonal threading all the way around the area.

6. To work the *head section,* follow this sequence (see Fig. 105). Tie your thread at brad 58; pull across to brad 32; work a twisting effect in a counter-clockwise direction: 32-57; 57-31; 31-56; 56-30; 30-55; 55-29; 29-54; 54-28; 28-53; 53-27; 27-52; 52-26; 26-51; 51-25; 25-50; 50-24; 24-49; 49-23; 23-48; 48-22; 22-47; 47-21; 21-46; 46-20; 20-45; 45-19; 19-44; 44-18; 18-43; 43-17; 17-42; 42-16; 16-41; 41-15; 15-40; 40-14; 14-39; 39-13; 13-38; 38-12; 12-37; 37-11; 11-36; 36-10; 10-35; 35-9; 9-34; 34-8; 8-33; 33-7; 7-32. Tie off.

Work this sequence first in green and then in blue. If you wish, you can continue working this threading sequence until you achieve an effect that pleases you.

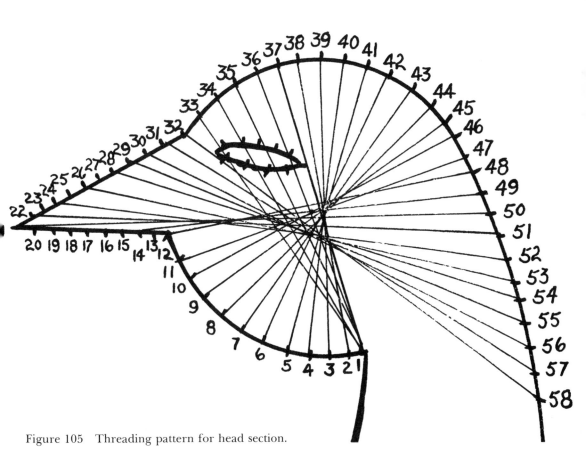

Figure 105   Threading pattern for head section.

7.   The *lower area under the face section* (see Fig. 106) is worked as follows: 1-12; 12-2; 2-11; 11-3; 3-10; 10-4; 4-9; 9-5; 5-8; 8-6; 6-7. Tie off.

8.   To work the *eye and beak section,* follow this sequence (see Fig. 106). The eye is simply outlined with brads which are then used to complete the threading in this section. Tie your thread at brad 1 on the eye and follow this sequence: 1-35; 35-2; 2-34; 34-3; 3-33; 33-4; 4-32; 32-5; 5-29; 29-5; 5-25; 25-6; 5-27; 27-6; 6-23; 23-6; 6-19; 19-6; 6-17; 17-1; 7-25; 25-7; 7-23; 23-8; 8-21; 21-9; 9-19; 19-9; 9-17; 17-10; 10-15. Tie off.

This threading is first worked in beige thread and then white, for fuller, layered effect.

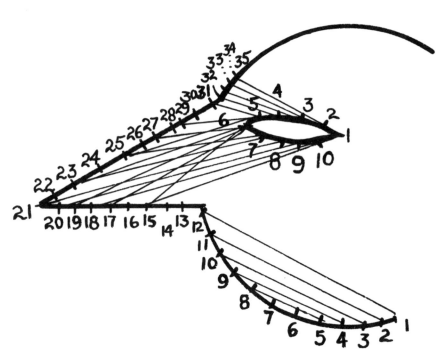

Figure 106   Threading pattern for chin and beak.

Three-Dimensional Designs

A whole new form of expression in string art can be created with three-dimensional designs, using the same basic principles and guidelines we've discussed here.

Three-dimensional designs have been used for years in home decorating and furnishing. In the craft and hobby areas, as well as the home furnishing industry, engineers and designers have developed some attractive materials such as copper, aluminum, and Plexiglas® that are excellent for use in string art designs.

Plexiglas is a rigid, resilient, acrylic sheet. It is readily available in various sizes, colors, and thicknesses throughout the country. Detailed literature on how to use Plexiglas in the home, including descriptive pictures on how to scribe, break, cut, and finish it, is available from the Rohm and Haas Company, Philadelphia, Pa. 19105.

Desk Accent Piece

The three-dimensional table or Desk Accent piece shown in the color section is made of Plexiglas, nylon filament, and a wooden base. The threading is worked in a one-to-one correspondence method. The Plexiglas is a clear, 8″ semi-circular piece mounted on a rectangular wooden base, 8″ × 2″.

Nails must be hammered into the wooden base and grooves must be made in the Plexiglas to hold the threading. The Plexiglas must have the same number of grooves as there are nails in the wooden base; the grooves and the nails must all be evenly spaced apart.

Both sides of the piece are worked simultaneously. The filament is tied at one side, threaded across the slits on the Plexiglas, looped around the brads on the wooden base, and pulled back across the slits to the opposite side of the base. Follow this sequence to complete the threading.

Figure 107   Three-dimensional Mobile design.

Mobile

Pleasing and attractive three-dimensional designs of all shapes can be made with dowels or wooden picture frames. Dowels are available at lumberyards in various lengths and widths. You can either hammer small brads into the dowel or make slits to hold the thread.

If dowels are used, cut the ends of each piece at a 45 degree slant for proper fitting. Hobby, wood, or airplane glue can be used to join the dowels.

These three-dimensional designs must be well executed and materials and threading patterns must be well chosen because the finished project will be seen from all sides. A variety of threads and wire can be used to produce interesting designs.

The Mobile shown in Figure 107 is made from a rectangular picture frame, 24" × 30". Brads must be hammered on all four edges. By the nature of a rectangle, you will have more brads on the longer sides than the shorter sides if the brads are evenly spaced. If you would like to have the same number of brads on all four edges so that you can work the one-to-one threading pattern for a simple design, space the brads on the shorter edges closer together than those on the longer edges.

On the other hand, you may want to work a more lively pattern for the three-dimensional effect. A twisting threading pattern is quite effective in a three dimensional design.

The design in Figure 107 is threaded with copper wire and red crochet thread with brass brads and is worked with the same number of brads on each edge.

Starting in the upper left corner, pull diagonally to the lower right corner. Now, work your threading in a clockwise direction to form an X pattern in the center of the frame. Now, work the left and bottom edges in a one-to-one correspondence pattern; then the top and right sides in a one-to-one pattern.

After some practice with three-dimensional string art, you will be able to create an infinite number of intricate and interesting designs, using a variety of frames and threading patterns.

ROBERT E. SHARPTON, a mathematics professor at Miami-Dade Community College, Miami, Florida, has a diverse and rich background in both the academic and professional fields. He spent six years with the Department of State, Fulbright Commission in Iran, and Lebanon, working in mathematics and science education with the Ministry of Education. He then lectured at the University of Maryland during the summer of 1969 and has worked as a consultant in the field of instructional technology.

Bob has studied in both the United States and abroad. He holds a BS degree from Central State University, Ohio, in chemistry/mathematics, an MA degree from Michigan State University, and is currently a PhD candidate at Michigan State Univeristy in the field of instructional technology in mathematics for the visually handicapped. His 1972-73 academic year was spent at Michigan State University as a Ford Fellow. Bob has received several national fellowships in the areas of science, mathematics, journalism, and instructional technology.

Over the past three years, several national magazines have published Bob's string craft designs. An article, "Doing the String Thing," was published by *Design* in midwinter 1972. Bob wrote a string craft article for the August 1972 issue of *Creative Crafts,* and the design appeared on the magazine's cover. *Creative Crafts* also published a how-to string craft article of Bob's, entitled "Yule String Along," in its December 1972 issue. In January 1972, Cunningham Art Products, Inc., published a set of his designs, *Designing in String,* in their Royal-Craft Library. Bob is also the author of a book for vocational education and industrial arts students, *Designing Pictures with String,* that was published by Emerson Books, Inc., in 1974.

Bob has given several local television demonstrations and has instructed teachers, doctors, engineers, and elementary through college level mathematics classes on the techniques of stringing pictures using a mathematical, as well as an artistic, approach to the craft.

Bob is also a professional model in both fashion and commercial work.